Lea...
Exp...

Tony Kippenberger

■ Fast track route to understanding leaders and leadership

■ Covers the key areas of leadership, from transformational, charismatic and adaptive leadership to co-leadership and a new emphasis on great low-profile leaders

■ Examples and lessons from some of the world's most successful leaders, including Jack Welch, Akio Morita, and Archie Norman, and ideas from the smartest thinkers, including Warren Bennis, Manfred Kets de Vries, Charles Hampden-Turner and Fons Trompenaars, Henry Mintzberg, and Jim Collins

■ Includes a glossary of key concepts and a comprehensive resources guide

>> EXPRESS EXEC.COM <<
essential management thinking at your fingertips

LEADING

10.06

Copyright © Capstone Publishing 2002

The right of Tony Kippenberger to be identified as the author of this work has been asserted in accordance with the Copyright, Designs and Patents Act 1988

First published 2002 by
Capstone Publishing (a Wiley company)
8 Newtec Place
Magdalen Road
Oxford OX4 1RE
United Kingdom
http://www.capstoneideas.com

All rights reserved. Except for the quotation of short passages for the purposes of criticism and review, no part of this publication may be reproduced, stored in a retrieval system, or transmitted, in any form or by any means, electronic, mechanical, photocopying, recording or otherwise, without the prior permission of the publisher.

CIP catalogue records for this book are available from the British Library and the US Library of Congress

ISBN 1-84112-359-5

This book is printed on acid-free paper

Substantial discounts on bulk quantities of Capstone books are available to corporations, professional associations and other organizations. Please contact Capstone for more details on +44 (0)1865 798 623 or (fax) +44 (0)1865 240 941 or (e-mail) info@wiley-capstone.co.uk

Contents

Introduction to ExpressExec

ExpressExec is 3 million words of the latest management thinking compiled into 10 modules. Each module contains 10 individual titles forming a comprehensive resource of current business practice written by leading practitioners in their field. From brand management to balanced scorecard, ExpressExec enables you to grasp the key concepts behind each subject and implement the theory immediately. Each of the 100 titles is available in print and electronic formats.

Through the ExpressExec.com Website you will discover that you can access the complete resource in a number of ways:

» printed books or e-books;
» e-content – PDF or XML (for licensed syndication) adding value to an intranet or Internet site;
» a corporate e-learning/knowledge management solution providing a cost-effective platform for developing skills and sharing knowledge within an organization;
» bespoke delivery – tailored solutions to solve your need.

Why not visit www.expressexec.com and register for free key management briefings, a monthly newsletter and interactive skills checklists. Share your ideas about ExpressExec and your thoughts about business today.

Please contact elound@wiley-capstone.co.uk for more information.

Introduction to Leadership

Does leadership matter? How much difference does it really make? Chapter 1 explains:

» why it has been important to humankind through the ages; and
» the big difference it can make to organizational success or failure (with two examples).

"Leadership is often . . . the single most critical factor in the success or failure of institutions."

Bernard Bass, US academic and psychologist

Leadership has been with us since our distant forebears, the nomadic hunter-gatherers, when survival depended on someone's ability to lead successful hunting expeditions or guide their wandering cluster of families from one dependable food source to another. Leadership, it seems, is part of the human condition. As a social animal, mankind is most comfortable in groups and where there are groups there are those that take a lead and those that are prepared to follow.

And so it has been down the ages. From wandering groups to migrating tribes, from hunters to farmers, from settlements to cities, from city-states to nations and empires, the difference between life and death, or at least between surviving or thriving, has depended – especially at critical moments – on successful leadership.

In the process, leadership has taken many forms – military, civic, and religious. And the emergence of leaders has occurred in many different ways – through democracy or by self-selection, by acclaim or by heredity, by mystical appointment or through the seizure of power.

In the business context, leadership comes in many forms – from the entrepreneur who starts up a business from scratch and leads it through its early, critical years, to the leader of a long-established firm who opens up new ways for future growth or development. Leaders and potential leaders exist at all levels of an organization, but nowhere are the qualities of leadership more critical than in the person at the helm of the enterprise.

So it should come as no great surprise that as the business world has become more intensely competitive, as the complexities of global markets have become apparent, and as yesterday's certainties have become tomorrow's unknowns, the demand for – and interest in – top level leadership has grown dramatically.

While this has brought with it all sorts of hype, there can be little doubt that any corporate leader can be a powerful force for either good or ill. And nowhere can this – and therefore the importance of leadership – be better illustrated than by the extraordinary irony in the contrasting fates of two long-established industrial giants which came to a head in September, 2001.

A TALE OF TWO LEADERS

In 1878 the Edison Electric Light Company was founded to develop Thomas Edison's work on "incandescent lamps." Eleven years later, after winning a key patent lawsuit, the Edison General Electric Company was formed in New York. In 1892, after merging with another electrical concern, it changed its name to the General Electric Company, or GE as it is commonly known today.

Meanwhile, in London two German immigrants, Gustav Byng and Hugo Hirst, established The General Electric Apparatus Company in 1886. Two years later they acquired their first factory in Manchester to manufacture telephones, electric bells, and switches, and in 1889 they changed the business' name to The General Electric Company, later to be better known as GEC.

On the two sides of the Atlantic these two companies, bearing the same name, thrived and grew throughout the twentieth century. Founded within a few years of each other at the start of the electricity revolution, they rode the waves of innovation that followed, introducing new products, extending their ranges, acquiring other businesses, and expanding overseas. Both became sprawling conglomerates. Both became the dominant force within their industry in their domestic markets. Both retained their name until, that is, GEC's name was changed to Marconi in 1999.

In the US, GE was led by a succession of eight internally appointed CEOs, each of whom brought their own different abilities to bear on the business. In the UK, GEC was dominated first by co-founder Hugo Hirst, who remained managing director until 1943, and then by Arnold Weinstock, who ran it for 33 years from 1963 until his retirement in 1996.

On Friday, September 7, 2001, GE's then CEO, Jack Welch, formally handed over to his hand-picked successor Jeffrey Immelt. In doing so, he passed on a business which, over the previous 20 years, had been transformed from the world's tenth largest conglomerate into the world's biggest business. Accolades for this achievement have been showered upon him. (See Chapter 7 for the full story.)

Just three days earlier, on September 4, George Simpson, Marconi's CEO, had been ignominiously ousted from his job, after a second profit-warning within two months, amid news of a further 2000 job losses to be added to the 8000 already announced.

Over his 20-year tenure, Jack Welch kept GE in much the same business areas but shifted the emphasis from products to services, drove for growth in international markets, and launched waves of internal initiatives designed to reinvigorate the company. In his five years in the job, George Simpson sold off much of the old GEC, refocussing instead on high-tech digital telecom networks–a strategy that involved costly acquisitions in the US, Australia, and Germany, funded by Weinstock's fabled cash mountain that had been built up in the 1980s, and the cash proceeds from the sale of GEC businesses.

Welch was loudly decried by commentators on all sides for his brutal downsizing of GE in his early years and GE's share price did little more than track US stock market indices for his first six years in the post. Simpson was widely acclaimed for his strategic change of direction and Marconi's share price soared to more than £12 at the height of the telecom boom in 2000.

But in those early days of September 2001 both men actually left behind very different track records. During Welch's period in office GE's share price had climbed from a little over $1 to more than $60. He had therefore overseen a massive creation of value as the company's market capitalization grew from $12bn in 1981 to some $485bn when he retired.

Having watched GEC/Marconi's shares rise from around £3 when he arrived to four times that value, Simpson left as they fell to just £0.29 – 10% of their value even three months earlier. His mistimed takeovers meant that the company had to write off £3.5bn in goodwill. Saddled with over £2bn of debt, its blue chip AA bonds reduced to junk bond status (trading for 25% of their face value), what had once been the UK's largest company was valued at less than £1bn.

For everyone involved with these two companies, in September, 2001, it was – to quote the opening line of Charles Dickens' *A Tale of Two Cities* – "the best of times and the worst of times." So don't let anyone persuade you that good or bad leadership, either now or in the future, is unimportant.

What is Leadership?

Most people think they understand the word "leadership," but there is no agreed definition of what it means. It can be an art, a process, or an attribute. Chapter 2 looks at ways to capture this elusive subject. It includes:

» different definitions;
» real-world observations of leaders; and
» possible contrasts between leaders and managers.

"Leadership is like beauty: it's hard to define, but you know it when you see it."

Warren Bennis, leadership expert

Warren Bennis, the pre-eminent leadership expert, succinctly sums up the problems associated with his chosen subject: "Without question, leadership is the most studied and least understood topic of any I can think of."

However, this lack of understanding is not for want of trying. American academics Bernard Bass and Ralph Stogdill first published their *Handbook of Leadership* in 1974, listing 3000 studies on the subject. By 1981, their second edition contained 5000 and the current edition – published in 1990 – contains 7000. Given the amount of literature produced on the subject in the last 10 years, no doubt any future edition will top the 10,000 mark.

Unfortunately, as many interested in the field will quickly point out, the popularity of the field of leadership is not matched by the relevance of the research conducted into it. Much of it is based on small, often inappropriate, samples, is pedestrian in quality, and detached from the real world in its findings.

Manfred Kets de Vries, professor of human resource management at the INSEAD business school in France, echoes the view of many when he says: "In the area of leadership, it seems that more and more has been studied about less and less."[1] Reading the existing literature on the subject is, he suggests, "rather like going through a Parisian telephone directory written in Chinese!"

DEFINING LEADERSHIP

Part of the problem is the absence of a commonly agreed definition. By the early 1980s Warren Bennis had already identified over 350 different definitions and, given the seemingly endless interest in the subject since, there will be many more by now.

Perhaps at its simplest, leadership can best be seen as the ability to get other people to achieve something that you wish them to accomplish. Certainly this basic theme lies at the heart of many long-standing definitions:

"Leadership is the ability to get men to do what they don't like to do and like it."

Harry S. Truman, President of the USA 1945-53

"Leadership is the art of influencing human behavior through an ability to directly influence people and direct them toward a specific goal."

General Omar N. Bradley, Chief of Staff, US Army (1948)

"Leadership can be defined as the process by which an agent induces a subordinate to behave in a desired way."

Warren Bennis (1959)

"Leadership is the process of influencing the activities of a group toward goal setting and goal achievement."

Ralph Stogdill (1974)

Although these four definitions effectively say the same thing, they also provide examples of the potential for hair-splitting that bedevils the leadership field. For example, they variously describe leadership as an "ability," an "art," and a "process." Is it one or all of these things? There is also, for instance, a significant difference between "influencing," which suggests persuasion, and "inducing," which indicates some level of authority or control. Semantic niceties play at least as much of a confusing role in the subject of leadership as they do in so many management areas.

Such definitions also emphasize the role of the leader, with little said about the followers and how their interests may be engaged. Other definitions seek to incorporate this missing element:

"Leadership is inducing followers to act for certain goals that represent the values and motivations - the wants and needs, the aspirations and expectations - of both leaders and followers."

James MacGregor Burns[2]

Yet other definitions widen the role of leadership significantly:

"Leadership is fundamentally about helping people 'make sense' of what they do so that they will understand and be committed to the mission of the organization; it is about finding ways to remind members who they are and why they are there; it is about creating a 'system' or 'culture' in which members instinctively do the 'right thing' even when the official leaders are absent."

William Drath and Charles Paulus[3]

Another area that has potential for confusion is the fact that leadership is seen as an activity as well as an individual attribute. This dichotomy is neatly resolved by Arthur Jago, professor of management at Yale University, who defines leadership as "both a process and a property. As a process, leadership is the use of non-coercive influence to direct and co-ordinate the activities of group members toward goal accomplishments. As a property, ... [leadership is a] characteristic attributed to those who are perceived to employ such influence successfully."[4] This last point also alludes to another aspect of leadership – its retrospective conferment, after the event. Australian author and leadership consultant, Alistair Mant, makes a similar point: "Leadership is what is attributed to a situation that has been successful."[5]

The trouble with definitions is that, in the end, they can become so fulsome and all-encompassing that they can confound rather than enlighten. For example, Dave Ulrich, professor of business administration at the University of Michigan's business school, provides an idealized list. Leadership, in his view, is "an art and a science. It involves change and stability, it draws on personal attributes and requires interpersonal relationships, it sets visions and results in actions, it honors the past and exists for the future, it manages things and leads people, it is transformational and transactional, it serves employees and customers, it requires learning and unlearning, it centers on values and is seen in behaviors."[6] So there you have it!

LEADERS IN THE REAL WORLD

Given that there is no one definition of leadership that is widely accepted, it is worth looking at the views of two authoritative figures who have spent a great deal of time talking to, meeting, and working with real-world leaders.

In *On Becoming a Leader*[7], Warren Bennis states that a wide range of leaders he had talked to in the US agreed on two basic points. "First, they all agree that leaders are made, not born, and made more by themselves than by external means." He also found that the leaders he had talked to showed little interest in proving themselves but did have a strong desire to express themselves. Bennis sees this as crucial: "it's the difference between being driven, as too many people are today, and leading, which too few people do."

Based on hundreds of conversations, Bennis argues that leadership is based on learning, learning from one's own life and experience, understanding one's self and the world. This also requires the ability to unlearn as much as to learn, to be able to reflect on, and draw lessons from, mistakes.

Peter Drucker, the doyen of management thinkers, in his foreword to *The Leader of the Future*[8] is categorical about the four things that the effective leaders he has met over his lifetime knew about leadership:

"1. The only definition of a leader is someone who has followers. Some people are thinkers. Some are prophets. Both roles are important and badly needed. But without followers, there can be no leaders.

2. An effective leader is not someone who is loved and admired. He or she is someone whose followers do the right things. Popularity is not leadership. Results are.

3. Leaders are highly visible. They therefore set examples.

4. Leadership is not rank, privileges, titles or money. It is responsibility."

He also identifies specific behaviors of effective leaders. They don't ask "what do I want?" - they ask "what needs to be done?" They then identify what they can do that will make a difference - choosing something that plays to their most effective strengths. Whilst they bear in mind the organization's goals all the time, they actually concentrate on what constitutes real performance and results. Tolerant of diversity, it doesn't cross their minds whether they like or dislike people, but they are intolerant of weak performance or poor standards and values. They enjoy being surrounded by strong colleagues and make sure that they are the person they want to be, with the self-respect and personal beliefs that enable them to avoid the temptation to be popular rather than right. Such effective leaders, in Drucker's view, are "doers," not preachers.

He believes, with Bennis, that, whilst there may be born leaders, "there surely are too few to depend on them. Leadership must be learned and can be learned."

MANAGERS AND LEADERS

Another way to capture something that proves so elusive is to define it by contrasting it with something else. Warren Bennis does precisely this when he says: "Managers do things right, leaders do the right things." This short dictum sounds familiar to anyone who has heard a similar contrast between efficiency and effectiveness. But Bennis, particularly in his early work, provides a long list of apparently definitive differences between managers and leaders.

Managers accept the status quo and so administer and maintain – taking a short-term view. They focus on systems, structure, and controls, and only ask how and when. The leader, on the other hand, has a long-term perspective and so innovates, develops, and originates – while focusing on people. He or she challenges, asks why, and inspires trust.

Few would question which is the rosier picture! Particularly when the manager is described as being the classic good soldier, while the leader is defined as his or her own person.

But in fact, at the start of the twenty-first century, much has been reversed. Many hands-on leaders are now likely to ask "when and how?" and many sophisticated followers, in our post-deferential age, are likely to ask "why?" Given the power of stock market sentiment and the attraction of this year's stock options, plenty of leaders take a short-term view, even though many of those working in the rest of the business plead for a longer-term perspective.

In any case, Alistair Mant points out that this desire to make a big difference between leaders and managers actually reflects a particularly American view of leadership – in Europe, for instance, few see the need to make such a big differentiation between the role of leading and managing.

KEY LEARNING POINTS

» There is no single agreed definition of leadership.
» At its simplest, it is about persuading others to help you achieve a common goal.
» It is more art than science, but it is also an ability, a process, and an attribute.
» Most leaders are made, not born - leadership can be learned.
» Americans draw a distinction between leaders and managers; others see this as an unnecessary dichotomy.

NOTES

1 Manfred Kets de Vries, *Life and Death in the Executive Fast Lane*, Jossey-Bass, 1995.
2 James MacGregor Burns, *Leadership*, Harper & Row, 1978.
3 William H. Drath and Charles J. Paulus, *Making common sense: leadership as meaning-making in a community of practice*, Center for Creative Leadership, Greensboro, NC, 1994.
4 Arthur G. Jago, "Leadership: Perspectives in Theory and Research," *Management Science*, vol. 28, March 1982, pp. 315-16.
5 Alistair Mant, *Intelligent Leadership*, Allen & Unwin, 1997.
6 Dave Ulrich, "Credibility × Capability" in *The Leader of the Future*, Jossey-Bass, 1996.
7 Warren Bennis, *On Becoming a Leader*, revised 2nd edition, Perseus, 1994.
8 *The Leader of the Future*, Frances Hesselbein, Marshall Goldsmith, Richard Beckhard (eds), Jossey-Bass, 1996.

The Evolution of Leadership Thinking

Philosophers, thinkers, and writers have wrestled with the subject for thousands of years. Chapter 3 examines how the concept of leadership has evolved and developed over time. It traces:

» ideas from ancient Chinese through to Renaissance times;
» theories investigated during the twentieth century; and
» the shift from authoritarian to democratic leadership in businesses.

"Leadership is one of the most observed and least understood phenomena on earth."

James MacGregor Burns, leadership expert and author

In tracing the evolution of thinking on the subject of leadership, a number of things stand out. One is the age-long fascination in the subject, a reflection of its deep significance to mankind's successful development and continued well-being. And, as an integral part of this, an undiminished interest in those characteristics that go to make for successful leadership.

The flip-side of the coin is the elusive nature of the subject, which makes such endeavors limited in their outcome – the repeated identification of the same attributes, few of which are exclusive to leaders. And, running parallel to this, the apparent futility of the search for a universally applicable model of leadership.

Despite thousands of years of leadership experience around the world, much of what works and what doesn't still remains a mystery.

EARLY CHINESE IDEAS

As might be expected of such an ancient civilization, some of the earliest ideas about leadership can be found in a Chinese text called *The Great Plan*, probably written around 1120BC. This stipulates that good leadership requires clear rules that should be applied with firmness or gentleness, depending on the circumstance. It also underlines that leaders must lead by example.[1]

Around 500BC, Confucius also emphasized the need for example-setting and defined what in today's jargon would be called "value-driven" leadership: "Lead the people with governmental measures and regulate them with laws and punishment, and they will avoid wrongdoing but will have no sense of honor and shame. Lead them with virtue and regulate them by the rules of propriety, and they will have a sense of shame and, moreover, set themselves right."

Whether Sun Tzu's *The Art of War* – probably written between 300 and 500BC – is the work of one man or several is a matter of debate, but the emphasis on leadership is strong. Important qualities include intelligence, trustworthiness, humaneness, courage, and sternness – each element having its own role to play.

THE CLASSICAL WORLD

On the other side of the world, first the Greeks and then the Romans experimented with different forms of leadership. In 360BC, the Greek philosopher Plato wrote in *The Republic* that good civic leadership required intelligence, an understanding of the nature of justice, wisdom, integrity, and an ability to keep personal self-interest and the interest of the state apart.

From 600BC to nearly AD500 the Romans tried out many different forms of leadership - kings, republican consuls, dictators, caesars, imperators, and emperors. For a thousand-year period one of the world's greatest empires proved unable to determine whether deification, heredity, military prowess, democratic vote, or noble position were suitable criteria for successful leadership. Unfortunately, each form of leadership threw up both strong, successful leaders and weak, paranoid, highly dysfunctional ones. Just like any system for picking winners is likely to do today.

BIRTHRIGHT

Whatever lessons the Greeks and Romans may or may not have learned were lost in the Dark Ages. From the middle of the first millennium to the latter part of the second, the most common basis for leadership - around the world - remained heredity. Kings, emperors, and their nobles claimed legitimacy by bloodline. Civil wars and family feuding were commonplace, but anyone who gained power quickly established some sort of prerogative for themselves and their heirs.

While remnants of this old dynastic approach to power remain - best exemplified by the royal families of countries like the UK, Spain, Thailand, and Japan - it is, perhaps surprisingly, a concept that continually reappears. The desire to bequeath success to one's heirs is sometimes overwhelming - witness the evolution of dynastic ruling families in republics like India and, more recently, Syria. Even in the US there are families who appear to lay some sort of dynastic claim to the presidency.

In corporate life, there is still a propensity to bring the next generation into the "family" business - even when it is publicly owned. Cadbury, Pilkington, and Forte are recent UK examples, but the same applies in France, Germany, and the US, as well as in many countries in Asia. Leadership expert Warren Bennis is quick to point out the problem: "As countless deposed kings and hapless heirs to great fortunes can attest, true leaders are not born, but made ..."

THE REALITIES OF LEADERSHIP

One of the earliest Europeans to look at the qualities of successful leadership with fresh eyes was Niccolò Machiavelli, whose views were published in *Il Principe* (*The Prince*) c.1513. He believed leaders needed a combination of characteristics. They had to be partly "fox" – crafty, manipulative, cunning – and partly "lion" – bold, steadfast, and brave. Over the next 300 years there were plenty of leaders who combined these attributes successfully – Elizabeth I of England being a prime illustration. Others failed on both counts, like Charles I who instead protested the "divine right of Kings," before ultimately losing his head at the end of the English Civil War.

In the late nineteenth century, German sociologist Max Weber wrestled with sources of authority and different organizational types. Wrongly seen as the person who idealized bureaucracy, Weber was in fact deeply worried about the cold rationalism inherent in a perfected bureaucratic system. He foresaw that a bureaucracy's rigid hierarchies and pre-set procedures could completely curtail the expression of human feelings, emotions, and understanding. He believed that the best foil for the excesses of bureaucracy was a revolutionary, charismatic leader – someone able to overturn the rationalism and conservatism of an established tradition or organization.

His prediction about bureaucracies was wretchedly fulfilled when Adolf Eichmann, sentenced to death by an Israeli court in 1962 for his part in the Holocaust, said in his own defense: "I was a good bureaucrat." Tragically, the charismatic leader who had taken over a highly efficient German bureaucracy was Adolf Hitler.

Nevertheless, Weber's views on the important role of charismatic leadership were retrieved from history in the 1970s and now form a significant school of thought on leadership qualities (see Chapter 6).

EARLY MANAGEMENT THEORY

It wasn't until the early twentieth century, when businesses began to grow rapidly, that they became an area worthy of specific study in themselves. Even then, when Frederick Winslow Taylor introduced his concept of scientific management, he concentrated almost exclusively on the division of work between workers and managers with little or nothing to say about leadership. At about the same time a French engineer, Henri Fayol, wrote what is probably the first "management" book entitled *Administration Industrielle et Generale*. But Fayol was more interested in authority and believed that "to manage is to forecast and plan, to organize, to command, to co-ordinate and control." The concept of "leading" did not figure.

In fact, as a lone, and female, voice in an era of authoritarian mass production, Mary Parker Follett was probably the first to write on the subject of leadership in a business context. She wrote essays, gave lectures, and even worked as a consultant during the first three decades of the twentieth century. Her thinking was well ahead of its time. She believed, for example, that leadership could be learned and that good leaders created an "invisible leader" in the form of a common purpose. She made the case for team working and giving people responsibility and saw the need for leaders to be visionary: "The most successful leader of all is one who sees another picture not yet actualized" – someone who can "open up new paths, new opportunities."[2] Her views, however, did not fit their time and her work became largely forgotten until the 1990s. When it was rediscovered, Warren Bennis found that her work, which predated his own early writings by at least 40 years, was "dispiritingly identical" to contemporary leadership theory.

"GREAT MAN" AND "TRAIT" THEORY

While Follett's work was being ignored, a male-dominated world persisted in its belief that great national or military leaders were born with greatness in them. Since the world would have been different if men such as Julius Caesar, William the Conqueror, or Napoleon Bonaparte had not become leaders when they did, it was a short step to believing that these great leaders could have assumed a leadership role at any other place or time in history and made a similarly big difference.

Thus began the hunt for the impossible. If a limited number of people were uniquely endowed with the abilities and traits that made them natural leaders, it must surely be a relatively simple task to identify what these traits were. Unfortunately, "trait theory" studies of the time found at least a hundred essential, but different, characteristics associated with such leaders.

At its most bizarre, trait theory even ventured into measuring human characteristics – leaders were believed to have wide-set eyes, and the gap between the nose and upper lip was seen as an indicator of leadership ability.[3] Thankfully, this particular line of inquiry was discarded when a large American study, into 400 effective leaders, simply concluded "they are either above average height or below." A truly remarkable finding!

It is estimated that, over a 50-year period, more than 300 studies were conducted without finding conclusive evidence of any universal traits that specifically applied to successful leaders. As Douglas McGregor, then Sloan Professor of Management at MIT, said in his seminal 1960 book, *The Human Side of Enterprise*: "Many characteristics which have been alleged to be essential to the leader turn out not to differentiate the successful leader from the unsuccessful ones. In fact, some of them – integrity, ambition, judgement, for example – are to be found not merely in the leader, but in any successful member of an organization." While it may be true that the limited number of pre-eminent leaders in any one field are also unusually gifted people, "they do not possess a pattern of leadership characteristics in common." As a result, trait theory had lost most of its momentum by the time of World War II, although it still raises its head from time to time even today.

WHAT ABOUT THE WORKERS?

While trait theory ran its course, the first flickerings of a challenge to deeply entrenched authoritarian attitudes started to emerge. Between 1924 and 1933, what became known as The Hawthorne Studies took place at one of Western Electric's factories near Chicago.

Elton Mayo, and his colleagues who undertook the studies, found that work satisfaction lay in recognition, security, and a sense of belonging, rather than their pay packets. It was a reflection of the times that people were surprised to find that treating workers as people rather than production machines improved motivation and commitment and this in turn improved productivity. From this small beginning emerged the "Human Relations School," which emphasized the benefits of a more participative and democratic way of managing.

Then, in 1938, Chester Barnard became one of the first experienced businessmen to set down the lessons he had learned as president of New Jersey Bell Telephone. In his influential book, *Functions of the Executive*, Barnard argued that to get the best out of people, business leaders would have to recognize that organizations were in fact co-operative systems and that successful leadership was all about inspiring that co-operation. This, in his view, could not be done by command and control alone. People needed to believe in a common purpose – something with which they could personally associate – before they committed to real co-operation with management. Today, finding such common cause would be called having a "vision."

At about the same time, German-born psychologist Kurt Lewin, one of the founding fathers of social psychology, published his research on leadership. Working at the University of Iowa, he and his colleagues had conducted experiments on three different forms of leadership, which are examined below.

Laissez-faire leader

Such a leader allows completely free rein to the group, maintaining a hands-off approach, not joining in discussions or making decisions, only offering advice when asked.

Autocratic leader

The autocratic leader is the decision-maker, issuing commands, setting tasks and time-scales. Control is maintained by selective praise, rewards or punishment. The autocrat is above the group and knows best.

Democratic leader

The democrat encourages group discussion and shared decision-taking, helps the group to formulate its goals, and then provides freedom over who works with whom and who does which tasks. Such a leader always seeks to be objective and fair and acts as if part of the group.

The results of the Iowa studies showed that, while the democratic approach was most popular, opinions were not unanimous. Lewin's findings were subsequently used to support a more democratic approach to business leadership. This despite the fact that its transposition to a business environment was never intended.

BEHAVIORAL STUDIES

Sadly these shifts to a more open, "democratic" form of leadership were shortly to be put on hold among the demands of wartime production. However, after World War II, with trait theory proving to be a blind alley, management research moved on to try and identify the behavior of successful leaders. During the 1950s and 1960s, researchers at Ohio State University and the University of Michigan undertook a range of studies to identify which behaviors worked best. They looked at how people responded to leaders who built trust by behaving sensitively toward them, respecting both their ideas and feelings. They then looked at leaders who put tasks before people, structuring work, defining group roles, setting deadlines, and imposing discipline.

By and large, the results indicated that, while people preferred the considerate leader, actual work performance, at least in the short term, was better under the task-oriented leader. Retrospectively, these studies were seen to have taken place at a time when military service was still obligatory and most workers were familiar with a command-and-control structure.

SITUATIONAL LEADERSHIP

So, by the 1960s, efforts to explain the phenomenon of successful leadership were running into the sand. Things were made worse by a growing recognition that political, military, and business leadership each had very different requirements – a fact borne out by post-war evidence that when leaders moved from one field to another they often failed in their new environment. With this came an acknowledgment that what makes for success in one historical period would probably not have worked in another. Furthermore, it was becoming apparent that a particular form of successful leadership was not necessarily transferable between cultures, industries, or even between different companies within the same industry.

As the search for the "one best way" petered out, attention began to switch to the context in which leadership took place. Clearly, not only were the characteristics of the leader important, but so too were the attitudes and needs of the "followers," the purpose, structure, and work undertaken by the organization, and even the wider social and economic environment of the time - especially the prevalent values. As Douglas McGregor put it, "the differences in requirements for successful leadership in different situations are more striking than the similarities."

While this sparked a new wave of interest in different styles of leadership (see *Leadership Styles* in the *ExpressExec* series), the failure of so much research to shed valuable light on the subject of leadership meant that during the 1970s interest in the subject dropped significantly.

THE REAWAKENING

While the appearance of aggressive corporate predators did something to stir boardrooms in the late 1970s, it was not until the alarm caused by the Japanese invasion of Western markets during the 1980s that interest in the subject was reawakened. In the US, articles and books on the art of Japanese management poured forth as, for the first time, American management methods were called sharply into question. At the top of the list of demands was an urgent need for a new dynamic form of business leadership, capable of shaking corporate America out of its complacent torpor. The hunt was on for a new type of charismatic, transformational leader - a search that continues today, as is explained in Chapter 6.

KEY LEARNING POINTS
» Importance has been attached to good leadership through the ages - such as by the Chinese, Greeks, and Romans.
» There are many ways to choose different types of leader, but none provides a guarantee that a selected leader will prove successful - e.g., the Romans.

» The long-established tradition of hereditary leadership continues today, but there is no evidence that leadership qualities are inherited – Bennis.

» Leadership can also have its dark side – e.g., Machiavelli.

» Charismatic leadership can be used to overturn tradition and conservatism – e.g., Weber.

» Dangers are inherent in charismatic leadership – e.g., Hitler.

» The concept of leadership was ignored in early management thinking – Taylor, Fayol.

» Concepts of teamwork, common purpose, and visionary leadership are not new – Follett, Barnard.

» No identifiable traits of successful leaders have been found – "great man" and "trait" theories.

» A shift from authoritarian to more democratic leadership began in the 1930s.

» Efforts to pinpoint successful leadership behaviors have been largely unsuccessful – Ohio and Michigan studies.

» Successful leadership depends on the specific context – situational leadership.

» Interest in the subject declined but was reawakened in the 1980s, initially in the US due to Japanese commercial success there.

NOTES

1 Violina P. Rindova and Willam H. Starbuck, "Ancient Chinese Theories of Control," *Journal of Management Inquiry*, 1997, 6, pp. 144-59.

2 Mary Parker Follett, *Dynamic Administration*, Elliot Fox and Lyndall Urwick (eds), Harper & Bros, New York, 1941.

3 Professor Gareth Jones, "The Leadership of Organizations," *Work & Leadership*, Gower, 1999.

The E-Dimension

Leadership has been changed by the digital revolution over the last 25 years. What are some of the ways the Internet will now make its impact? Chapter 4 explores some of the key issues. Among them:

» technological literacy;
» need for insights and speed; and
» the abiding importance of judgment.

"It is not the strongest of the species that survive, nor the most intelligent, but the ones most responsive to change."

Charles Darwin

Leadership in an increasingly electronic, digitally-connected, and net-worked world is already markedly different from leadership as it was practiced 25 years ago. But to understand how and why, it is important to put what has happened in context. The Internet – the thing that many people perceive as *the* e-dimension – is but the latest part of an information technology revolution that *as a whole* is continuing to change patterns of effective leadership.

Manuel Castells, highly respected sociologist and author of 20 books, traces what happened in his book *The Rise of the Network Society*, first published in 1996. In it he points out that information technology really took off in the 1970s, but then goes on to question why its subsequent diffusion was so rapid. One reason, it is clear, was a string of innovations in microelectronics, computing, and telecommunications that fed off each other – for example, computing performance increased about a million times between 1950 and 1990. But such innovation does not occur in a vacuum.

ORGANIZATIONAL CHANGE

This is because another trend, often forgotten in this context, was occurring at the same time. After the shock impact of the two oil crises of the 1970s, businesses in the US and Europe were suddenly confronted in the early 1980s by highly competitive incursions into their domestic markets by Japanese manufacturers. As a result, many companies were forced into making major changes in the ways they operated. On the one hand, there was a scramble to learn from the Japanese – introducing lean production and total quality management. And on the other, a drive to cut costs. This was done by stripping out layers of middle managers and introducing information technology to save labor and control production.

HORIZONTAL NETWORKS

But these hollowed-out companies were still vertical hierarchies – un-suited for newly flexible ways of working and increasingly volatile markets. So, over a 25-year period they have gone on adapting – organizing around processes not tasks, demolishing functional silos, and using cross-functional teams, constantly flattening the hierarchy. Under pressure, they have reached forward to customers, backward to suppliers, and sideways to collaborative partners – all in an endeavor to retain their markets. Meanwhile they have loosened the ties to their business units so they can respond more quickly. In the process the traditional boundaries, both between firms and within firms, have broken down and in their place a networked "horizontal corporation" has taken shape.

INTERDEPENDENCY

This organizational change, argues Castells, was only made possible by constant advances in information technology. But it has, he suggests, been a symbiotic relationship, because as new technologies have come along they have been shaped by the way in which they are used to enable organizational change. More than that, he believes the two are now locked in a mutual embrace that is molding them both as they evolve. And that is where the e-dimension of leadership comes in.

With a strong interdependency between IT, organizational design, and new ways of working, the recent arrival on the scene of a transformational infrastructure like the Internet will have a powerful and continuing impact, of much more significance than a brief surge of dot.coms. Leadership has adjusted over the last 25 years – less hierarchical, more visionary and inspirational, less command-and-control, more open and communicative. All this has been in response to changes in the way organizations, and the people within them, now have to operate. This process will now be dramatically shaped by new applications made possible by the Internet and the dynamics of a digitized economy.

OPEN, DEMOCRATIC, NON-HIERARCHICAL

In a June, 2001 speech, Carly Fiorina, CEO of Hewlett-Packard, underlined the point: "the Internet era has only just begun ... And, while the current economic slowdown has injected a bit of reality into some fairy-tale growth trajectories, we all know that the inherent value of the Internet is irrefutable. There's no going back. Fundamentally, it's a new form of communication: a form of communication that is open, democratic, immediate, non-hierarchical. The profound shift to a communications medium that is open, democratic, immediate, and non-hierarchical changes companies forever."[1] And, inevitably, the way they are led.

TECHNO-SAVVY

It is not long ago that it was commonplace for corporate leaders to have their assistants print out their e-mails for them and for a computer to sit silent on their desk. No doubt this still occurs, but it must be getting rarer by the week.

If organizational structures and IT are intertwined, the possibilities and ramifications of the Internet mean that strategy and leadership must now be caught up in their embrace. Where once strategy dictated what the IT department had to do, today it is what the Internet enables that is likely to determine strategy. And leaders who are technologically illiterate will be at a severe disadvantage.

In a recent article, appropriately entitled "Burying the Corps",[2] digital guru Don Tapscott points out that many business leaders still "fail to appreciate that the corporation itself is now obsolete as the starting point for strategic thinking. They must reinvent their business model with the Web at its core."

"INTERNETWORKERS"

Of course, the effect of the Internet on the way organizations will have to shape themselves remains an area of hot debate. Tapscott believes that the most dramatic effect is reduced transaction costs and it is this which will speed the already visible break-up of established organizational boundaries. Companies will disaggregate and then re-aggregate themselves into "business webs" – creating new business configurations which, through high levels of partnering, can provide extremely competitive offerings that fully integrated, traditional firms will find difficult to match.

Since such business webs are likely to be fluid – sometimes structured, sometimes amorphous – and may comprise different sets of participants or contributors, business leaders will need to be more than networkers, they will need to be *Internet* workers. Able to envisage new possibilities, conceive unique configurations, create special relationships, and then move quickly and decisively to change the way their business works.

Jack Welch, the highly respected leader of GE, castigated himself for being slow in understanding the significance of the Internet. But once he did, he famously launched a corporate-wide program called "destroyyourbusiness.com" to get all his business unit heads to think through the implications of the Internet for their businesses and sectors (see also Chapter 7).

E-LEVELED PLAYING FIELDS

The NASDAQ may have crashed and the dot.coms gone into meltdown, but if anyone thinks that all the possible applications of the Internet have now been tried and found wanting, they will be in for a shock. For example, because of the time lag in applications, the small and medium-sized enterprises (SMEs), that now comprise increasingly high proportions of both GNP and employment opportunities in the developed economies, have yet to take full advantage of the Internet. Innovative in their own right, well-adapted to flexible ways of working, and often entrepreneurially led, they are likely to be able to use the Internet to put themselves on much more equal terms with large-scale organizations.

E-JUDGMENT

As the smoke begins to clear from the "bonfire of the vanities" that consumed so many dot.com leaders (who put "greed" over "lead"), it is crystal clear that one aspect of leadership that will be in overwhelming demand in the future is "e-judgment."

The rush, the buzz, and the self-indulgent escapades of dot.commery can now be seen as the froth on the top of a bubble bath – in which many investors were taken to the cleaners. For all the talk that "pure-plays" would trounce old-style "bricks-and-mortar" companies, there is growing evidence that long-established corporate and leadership attributes – knowledge, experience, perseverance, and, above all, judgment – can pay off well in an e-world (see Tesco best practice case study below). B2B e-commerce is in its infancy – getting it right will require the insights and successful risk-taking that are the hallmark of effective leaders.

KNOWLEDGE-SHARERS

Within the organization, IT and especially the Internet have meant that – at least in theory – senior executives can dig and delve through their organization for information. Much of the latest software programming is directed at company-wide information flows – Enterprise Resource Planning being the archetype.

But the Internet, or more likely a corporate intranet, should also be a phenomenal means of sharing knowledge. David Simon, past chairman of BP, and John Browne, its current CEO, have worked hard to ensure that knowledge is shared worldwide within the company. To foster the sharing of knowledge, BP has created a complex network using video-conferencing, e-mail, intranet, and Internet that acts as a conduit for its dissemination. Information and knowledge can now be transferred in real time, and with ease, between business units that may be scattered across the globe from Alaska to Colombia, from Indonesia to the UK. In its first year alone (1996) it was estimated to have added $30mn of value to the company.

Leaders who build knowledge-sharing through IT and the Internet enable high-value skills transfer and ensure that they themselves are able to react quickly to unforeseen events.

E-VOIDING PEOPLE

In 1982, Peters and Waterman published their worldwide bestseller, *In Search of Excellence*, and in it one of the attributes of excellent companies was that the CEO understood MBWA – "management by walking about." Recent leadership theory has enjoyed changing the wording slightly – "walking the talk" – but the idea remains the same. Get out, meet, and talk to people!

Unfortunately, as reports of e-mail dismissal notices indicate, the new technologies provide a way of avoiding personal contact, let alone confrontation. Leaders have to recognize that the Internet and its associated technologies provide "mediated" communications rather than face-to-face reality. It is grand to disseminate mission statements, new goals, stretch targets over the Internet – via an intranet or e-mail – but this is no replacement for personal, direct contact. Highly effective leaders like Jack Welch know this well. He met his top 500 managers for a personal conversation and exchange of views, individually, every year – that is more than ten a week, on average. This is quite apart from the hundreds of other managers he talked to personally during the course of a year. As companies who have recently tried introducing "e-mail-free Fridays" have discovered, apparently to their surprise, electronic communication is no substitute for meeting and talking face-to-face.

E-TALENT RETENTION

Organizational capital today increasingly takes the form of knowledge and expertise. And knowledge workers are often much more influential and expect more intrinsic satisfaction from their work than their predecessors. In a world where speed, connectivity, real-time systems, and 24-hour accessibility are the order of the day, companies will need to find the energetic, flexible, and creative people who can act and respond rapidly. Empowering leadership, based on trust and valued relationships, will be critical.

In their 1999 book *Co-Leaders: The Power of Great Partnerships*, David Heenan and Warren Bennis reinforce the point: "The New Economy is characterized by camaraderie grounded in shared accomplishment. It is powered by teams of people working toward a common goal, doing exciting work, and doing it collaboratively. In this brave new world, one of the leadership's most important challenges is to understand and manage these multiple relationships as true partnerships. Leaders who fail to do so risk losing any organization's most important resource – its talent."

BEST PRACTICE – TESCO E-LEADERSHIP

1996 was an important year for Ian MacLaurin, head of UK supermarket giant Tesco. It was the year that he achieved his long-term goal of overtaking Tesco's rival, Sainsbury, to become the UK's most profitable supermarket operator. It was also the year in which he confirmed that he would be passing the helm on to his little-known successor, Terry Leahy, within 12 months.

In the same year Gary Sargeant, a former store manager, was put in charge of the company's embryonic online business – Tesco Direct. Based on his extensive grocery retailing experience, Sargeant felt that customers would prefer to purchase online from the store in which they would normally shop in person. Tesco customers were familiar with what was in their local store and knew the prices they normally paid. As a result, Tesco developed a model in which ordered items would be picked from the store's shelves and then delivered. Early experiments in London stores began and, by the end of 1996, Tesco was making 70 online deliveries a week – a very small beginning.

Meanwhile, on the other side of the Atlantic, Internet fever had begun and soon competitors were pouring into the new market "space" of home shopping. Groceries were in the vanguard, largely because Peapod, a company originally set up in 1989, had been one of the very first e-commerce companies in the world. Others – like Homeruns.com – now followed its lead, also building centralized distribution depots from which to make deliveries.

In 1998, another newcomer, Webvan, announced plans to build huge warehouses from which to distribute groceries across large metropolitan areas in the US. Throughout 1999, Webvan was constantly in the headlines, raising hundreds of millions of dollars in venture capital, announcing a $1bn order for automated warehouses and attracting George Shaheen, the managing partner of Andersen Consulting, to become its CEO. Shaheen promised to "reinvent the grocery business" and, shortly after its IPO in

November of that year, Webvan's stock price soared to well over $30, valuing the company at over $4bn.

Meanwhile, Tesco was gradually rolling out its store-based model, using its logistical expertise to iron out problems – such as delivery times and product availability – as it went. By early 2000, only 100 of its stores were offering online ordering and many commentators argued that it was using the wrong model and being too slow. However, as the year progressed, the learning process continued as more and more stores moved online, and newer and better technologies were adopted.

As a result, in April, 2001, Tesco.com was able to announce that online sales for the year had doubled to £237mn and were running at £300mn a year on an annualized basis. With 250 stores now involved, the company justifiably claimed to be the world's most successful online grocery retailer, handling 700,000 orders a week from a customer base of one million. Expenditure over the five-year period had been just £40mn.

In the same month, George Shaheen stepped down as CEO of Webvan, as the company's share price sank to $0.12. Three months later, Webvan filed for bankruptcy, having burned through an estimated $830mn. The same week Homeruns.com also closed.

Tesco's success had come, despite many siren voices, from persevering with its original model, and Caroline Bradley, the company's chief operating officer, puts that down to the personal backing of Terry Leahy, Tesco's low-key chief executive. An altogether quieter form of leadership than Shaheen's, but one solidly based on experience, trust, and judgment.

KEY LEARNING POINTS

» The Internet is a recent addition to a continuing digital revolution – Castells.
» That revolution has already made huge changes to organizations, the way we work, and the role of leadership over the last 25 years – Castells.

> » The Internet's impact on all these things will be big and long-lasting - Fiorina.
> » Strategy and technological possibilities are increasingly ent-wined - technologically illiterate leaders will not survive - Tapscott.
> » Leaders will have to move quickly and decisively to change the way their business works - Tapscott.
> » But the best leadership characteristics (knowledge, experi-ence, and judgment), when correctly applied, are still critical attributes - Tesco.
> » How leaders use the Internet is crucial - BP (knowledge-sharing).
> » Hiding behind electronic communication is no substitute for personal contact - Welch.
> » The war for talent will get no easier - Heenan and Bennis.

NOTES

1 Carly Fiorina, Santa Clara, June 23, 2001. A transcript of the speech can be found at: http://www.hp.com/hpinfo/execteam/speeches/fiorina/tiecon_01.htm.

2 Don Tapscott, "Burying the Corps," *Director Magazine*, August 2001.

The Global Dimension

Despite the hype, organizations are still anchored in their national origins and culture. But to succeed in the future, what will global leaders have to do? Chapter 5 looks at the challenges they now face. These include:

» multicultural leadership;
» cross-cultural collaboration;
» promoting diversity;
» ethical leadership; and
» mastery of communication.

"Leaders at the helm of the corporations of the future will need the capacity to step out of their comfort zone and adapt to other realities. The ability to speak more than one language well is a sign of that capacity."

Manfred Kets de Vries, academic and psychoanalyst

In 1983, marketing guru Theodore Levitt wrote an article in *Harvard Business Review* entitled "The Globalization of Markets." In it he conjured up a picture of a corporate utopia, one in which global companies who viewed the world as a single entity, selling "the same thing in the same way everywhere," would overtake old-style multinationals that had concentrated on local consumer preferences. In his view, the world's needs and desires would increasingly become "irrevocably homogenized."

To judge by the anti-globalization protests that now greet global leaders' meetings – like the WTO in Seattle, the European summit in Gothenburg, and the G8 summit in Genoa – you would think that Levitt's dream had come true. For instance, the only common thread that the *Financial Times* could find among the myriad protesters at Seattle was "a profound hostility to the global corporation." But the reality is that Levitt's globalization – in the sense of truly global corporations operating in a homogenized world environment – remains largely fictitious.

But within this dangerous mix of myth and reality lie many of the biggest implications for business leadership. It raises issues of cross-cultural understanding, international relationships, workforce diversity, ethics, and multicultural communications. To name but a few.

NATIONAL ANCHORS

Manuel Castells argues in his recent trilogy, *The Information Age*, that the global economy is not yet truly global–not least because "multi-national corporations still keep most of their assets and their strategic command centers in their historically defined 'home nations'." This view is reinforced by a 1998 US study,[1] *The Myth of the Global Corporation*, which argued that the way in which individual multinational companies act still heavily reflects the varied historical backgrounds in which they are rooted. Before a company can develop into a multinational, it has to be legally established, financed, and regulated under some national jurisdiction or other. Immediately, therefore, it starts life with a national character that will set the tone for its future activity.

Anchored within national or regional regulatory structures and headquartered in their own domestic economies, most leaders are totally familiar with their own national culture (and what that means in terms of communication, work ethic, work/life balance, etc.). But this is inadequate knowledge for the leadership of businesses operating on a global scale.

Gert Hofstede, the renowned Dutch expert on culture, makes the point clearly: "Whatever a naïve literature on leadership may give us to understand, leaders cannot choose their styles at will; what is feasible depends to a large extent on the cultural conditioning of a leader's subordinates."

MULTICULTURAL LEADERSHIP

After 15 years of continuous research into the subject, Fons Trompenaars and Charles Hampden-Turner are experts in cultural diversity. In their view, understanding cultural differences is critical to business and they warn that, since the US is the principal source of much management theory, it is essential to recognize that "favorite American solutions do not always solve the dilemmas of other nations."[2]

One of the biggest problems is cultural stereotyping. For example, Americans tend to stereotype the French as arrogant, flamboyant, hierarchical, and emotional, while the French often see Americans as naïve, aggressive, unprincipled, and workaholic. Leaders have to be increasingly cosmopolitan in their outlook so that they can avoid such easy typecasting (see "Global research" in Chapter 6).

Leaders also need to be able to recognize different value systems. The rule-based, conforming cultures of the developed West are markedly different from the personal relationship approach that is so important in Asia and South America. The individualistic attitudes so commonplace in Canada, the US, and Denmark are potentially at odds with the common goal (communitarian) approach that is found in Japan, China, and France. For example, something as simple as pay-for-performance will be viewed quite differently within each of these value systems.

Leaders of companies that span different cultures need to develop a strong sense of such systems, and the many other differences that can so easily lead to the misunderstandings that can block the workings of effective organizations.

CULTURAL AFFINITY

Manfred Kets de Vries, of INSEAD, believes that effective global leaders need a "healthy dose of interpersonal and transcultural sensitivity."[3] Many of the best European business leaders he has met – "globetrotting top executives" – have a remarkable understanding of the economic and cultural history of the countries in which they operate. But, for the future, they will need a genuine cultural affinity – a curiosity about how people live, combined with the ability to listen and observe well.

American social psychologist Ellen Langer, of Harvard University, flags up one of the great barriers to achieving such affinity – our "mindlessness."[4] That is, the human tendency to operate on autopilot. We all do it to an astonishing degree. She identifies the following three types of mindlessness.

» Categorization – we quickly categorize things we see and hear, often because we don't see things and then define them, rather we define things first and then see what we expected to see. For many people, groups of foreign nationals all look alike!
» Single perspective – we tend to go with the flow, for example leaving our minds in neutral as we drive along a familiar route. We are what psychologists call "cognitive misers," saving our mental energy for when it is needed, so we switch off and go onto autopilot.
» Repetitive habits – this is our propensity to form habits in our social behavior or in the way we do things. Acting automatically without thinking about what we are doing is our way to speed things up. Research shows that if we are asked to stop and think about what we're doing, we slow up a lot.

All this means we spend a lot of time taking in and using only limited signals from the world around us. We allow established mindsets and our preconceptions to do the work for us. Leaders in a culturally diverse world will have to develop "mindfulness," the ability to be attentive to what is actually happening and to view it in new ways and respond appropriately – not just out of habit.

LEADING PARTNERSHIPS

In a networked global economy, companies enter into more and more partnerships or joint ventures – many of which are formed with companies from different cultures. Harvard professor Rosabeth Moss Kanter argues that successful partnerships are analogous to marriage[5] – they are relationships that need nurturing – and leaders who are able to create and sustain such relationships give their company a valuable "collaborative advantage."

In her view, this relationship approach to business represents a major challenge to corporate America, where the traditional "adversarial" way of doing business is based on a deeply ingrained belief in self-reliance and a fear of being dependent on anyone else. Partnerships are not determined by sterile logic, but by senior executives establishing good personal relationships in which trust and mutual understanding can develop. In a global environment this requires the cross-cultural social skills identified by Kets de Vries.

INSIGHTFUL LEADERSHIP

Not only are cultures different, but also whole ways of working within national infrastructures vary significantly from one country to another. To succeed, global leaders have to gain insights and constantly widen their understanding of how others' cultures and nationalities operate – whether to compete or collaborate.

In a book published in 1996, two experts on Japan, Kenichi Miyashita and David Russell,[6] describe how Japanese managers forgive Western manners – walking on the *tatami* (straw mats) with their shoes on or presenting their business cards upside down. But what these Japanese managers, who study American and European companies so assiduously, cannot understand is the staggering ignorance – particularly among US companies – of the way Japanese business operates. Future global leaders will pay a heavy price for such ignorance.

DIVERSITY

In the past, Western multinationals' approach to emerging markets has tended to be almost exclusively from their own domestic perspective, seeing them simply as markets, with little real empathy for the new customers' needs and desires. American management academics C.K. Prahalad and Kenneth Lieberthal, both from the University of Michigan, accuse such companies of "corporate imperialism"[7] and argue that, until this mindset is changed, multinational corporations cannot hope to gain real competitive advantage in the critical markets like India and China.

One of the big problems is that the vast majority of senior managers in multinational corporations come from the "home country." But Prahalad and Lieberthal predict that in 10 years' time up to 30% or 40% of the top team in multinational companies will have to come from countries like China, India, and Brazil – the big new markets. What they question is whether companies and their leaders will be ready to cope with such diversity at top executive level.

BEST PRACTICE

One company that is setting an example is the multicultural, Anglo-Dutch consumer products company Unilever. Unilever's chairman, Niall Fitzgerald, appointed Keki Dadiseth, chairman of the company's Indian subsidiary Hindustan Lever, to a main board position in charge of personnel worldwide in May, 2000. In January, 2001, Unilever split itself into two units and Dadiseth became global division director of home and personal care products – half of Unilever's entire worldwide operations.

ETHICS

The most obvious form of globalization is the shift of production from high- to low-cost economies. For example, in recent years ABB has shed 40,000 jobs in Europe and added 45,000 in Asia, while Philips now has more Chinese workers than Dutch.[8]

This shift has brought with it many ethical issues. Sports shoe manufacturer Nike has suffered from accusations of poor working conditions and low wages in the countries where it outsources manufacturing, while charging high prices at the retail end. Similar pressures persuaded companies like Levi Strauss and GAP to devote considerable resources to identifying the first link in the supply chain (the suppliers to their suppliers), and to bring direct pressure to establish minimum wage standards and working conditions. The problems are, however, not simple – accepted working age is often dramatically lower in poor countries and social/cultural issues impinge on how poor families earn anything at all.

Global leaders will continually have to find ways to deal with multiple stakeholders, and the complexities they represent, at a world level. It is a difficult juggling act that requires clear values and ingrained ethical standards.

COMMUNICATION LEADERSHIP

But global leadership is more than just believing oneself to be a good global citizen. To quote the late Robert Half – leading recruitment consultant and founder of Robert Half International Inc. – "convincing yourself does not win an argument." Leaders have to take the lead in an increasingly global communications flow. And that means staying attuned to shifts in popular perceptions.

In 1991, the Brent Spar oil storage facility, a 40-storey, 14,000-ton North Sea oil platform, became obsolete. Its owner, Shell, looked at 13 possible options and undertook some 30 studies to determine the best alternative, before deep-sea disposal was chosen, a scheme approved by the UK government and the European Commission in Brussels.

What nobody had anticipated was that environmental activists Greenpeace were casting around for a *cause célèbre* to highlight hazardous discharges into the North Sea. In April, 1991, Greenpeace managed to occupy the rusted and deserted hulk in an act, carried out at sea, which immediately attracted media attention, cleverly reinforced by direct television feeds from Greenpeace to broadcasters around the world.

Over the next few weeks, Greenpeace footage of water cannons being used to evict the occupants made headline news. Each time, the perception deepened that Europe's largest company was using aggressive, potentially highly dangerous tactics on a small, dedicated band of men and women.

A boycott of Shell products began in several European countries, and in Germany, where Shell's sales had fallen by 20-30%, one Shell petrol station was bombed and another hit by a hail of bullets. Yet with feelings running this high, Shell still held to a rational approach, arguing its scientific and economic case largely through the print media. But, when the German chancellor, Helmut Kohl, protested to the UK prime minister, John Major, at the June 1991 G7 Summit, it was evident that the issue was moving outside Shell's control.

On June 20, as Brent Spar reached its final destination, John Major stood up in the UK parliament to defend his government's backing for Shell's chosen course of action. To his considerable chagrin, a few hours later Shell issued a short press release rescinding its decision, and began towing Brent Spar back toward the UK.

Subsequently, Greenpeace acknowledged that some of its case was based on incorrect information, but the point remained that Shell lost the argument. Corporate leaders have to come to terms with the power of global NGOs like Greenpeace and learn to cope with a world in which instant communication can affect their business anywhere in the world.

BEST PRACTICE - ABB'S GLOBAL LEADERS

During the 1990s, Percy Barnevik was showered with awards and accolades for the way in which he had transformed two electrical engineering giants - Brown Boveri of Switzerland and ASEA of Sweden - into a single fleet-of-foot global company employing over 200,000 people in more than 130 countries. The company, ABB (Asea Brown Boveri), more than doubled its revenues to $34bn over the period 1988-96.

Using a complex matrix structure that included no less than 5000 profit centers, ABB employed around 25,000 managers worldwide. With an executive committee of only 10 and a head office staff of less than 200, ABB depended on 500 "global managers" to run its global operations. What did Barnevik look for in these global leaders? What was ABB's best practice in global leadership?

» Primarily he looked for people he believed could become "superstars," tough-skinned, fast on their feet, action-oriented, and with a demonstrable ability to lead others.
» But he also knew they needed "patience, good language ability, stamina, work experience in at least two or three countries, and, most important, humility and respect for other cultures."[9]
» They had to have exceptionally open minds, have respect for how different countries did things, and the imagination to understand why they did them that way. But they must also be able to push at cultural preconceptions, refusing to accept cultural excuses when there were ways to improve and innovate.
» But, in Barnevik's own words, "... beyond all these characteristics they need another quality: do they develop their people? Is the person a 'giver' or 'receiver?' The giver makes people available to other parts of the organization; the receiver needs people all the time."

This latter point was essential to Barnevik's own global leadership. Despite early criticism, ABB were very fast in expanding into eastern Europe immediately after the fall of the Berlin Wall in 1989 – at one point the company was making one acquisition a month. The reason why they were able to move into such a culturally unfamiliar territory so successfully was that Barnevik had, some years earlier, recruited "locals" with managerial potential from Eastern Bloc countries. They had been working in ABB companies in the US, Germany, and Sweden and, well-trained and familiar with ABB's culture, they were available immediately to run ABB's new subsidiaries back in their home territory.

Having the right people available for the right tasks was an essential part of Barnevik's strategy. He knew that local managers always feel more comfortable with people of their own nationality on their team, but he constantly pushed them to look for people from other countries. In order to do that, good people from other countries had to be available. Hence the importance attached to "givers" not "receivers."

By 1997, ABB was employing over 80,000 people in emerging economies in eastern Europe and Asia. Barnevik's view was that, while many companies believed they could simply export from Europe or America, to be a truly global business required ABB to establish itself locally.

In Barnevik's view, global managers or leaders are made, not born.[10] It is not a natural process, because humans are like herd animals - we like people who are like us. So, in his view, it is best practice to grow such leaders within the organization and constantly expose them to different cultures and nationalities - that way, global leadership can be learned.

KEY LEARNING POINTS

» Despite "globalization," companies remain anchored to their national identities and cultures - Castells and others.
» Understanding different cultural value systems is critical to business leadership in a global context - Trompenaars, Hampden-Turner.
» Acquiring real cultural affinity by being "mindful" will be a requirement for the future - Kets de Vries, Langer.
» Cross-cultural collaboration requires cross-cultural social skills - Kanter, Kets de Vries.
» Business leaders have to understand how companies in different cultures operate if they are to compete successfully - Japan.
» Welcoming a diversity of nationalities and cultures into the top management team will be the mark of a progressive company - Prahalad, Lieberthal, Unilever.
» Sustaining values and high ethical standards will continue to grow in importance - Nike, Levi Strauss, GAP.
» Leaders have to recognize the power of global NGOs and their ability to communicate fast and effectively - Greenpeace, Shell.
» Global leadership skills can be learned - Barnevik.

NOTES

1 Paul N. Doremus, William W. Keller, Louis W. Pandy, and Simon Reich, *The Myth of the Global Corporation*, Princeton University Press, 1998.
2 Fons Trompenaars and Charles Hampden-Turner, *Riding the Waves of Culture*, Nicholas Brealey Publishing, 1999.
3 Manfred Kets de Vries, *Life and Death in the Executive Fast Lane*, Jossey-Bass, 1995.
4 Ellen Langer, *Mindfulness*, Addison-Wesley, 1989.
5 Rosabeth Moss Kanter, "Collaborative Advantage," *Harvard Business Review*, July–August, 1994.
6 Kenichi Miyashita and David Russell, *Keiretsu: Inside the Hidden Japanese Conglomerates*, McGraw-Hill, 1996.
7 C.K. Prahalad and Kenneth Lieberthal, "The End of Corporate Imperialism", *Harvard Business Review*, July–August, 1998.
8 *Ibid.*
9 Manfred Kets de Vries, *The New Global Leaders*, Jossey-Bass, 1999.
10 Piero Morisini, *Managing Cultural Differences*, Pergamon Press, 1998.

The State of the Leadership Debate

There are so many ideas about what constitutes good leadership that they are best seen as a wide spectrum of opinion. Some are well-established threads, others are emerging views. How do they differ? Who are some of the main protagonists? Chapter 6 includes:

» transformational and charismatic leadership;
» adaptive leadership;
» leaders as builders and/or learners;
» co-leadership;
» quieter, more humble forms of leadership; and
» how dysfunctional leaders affect organizations.

"The extent to which Americans need heroes is absolutely mind-blowing."

Henry Mintzberg, Canadian academic and iconoclast

As might be expected with a sexy subject like leadership, there are many different schools of thought. Most are American in origin. Partly this is a result of the sheer scale of management research that is conducted in the US, but it also reflects that element of the American psyche that yearns for strong, sometimes "heroic," leadership.

For all the arguments that leadership is an ability that can be learned and developed, there remains a nostalgic hope that great leaders do emerge, born to the role, ready to take the helm and change everything for the better. While practically everyone agrees that from time to time this does occur, in business as in other spheres, there are plenty who argue that such a desire to pin everything on a single person is unrealistic, if not downright unhealthy.

To understand where the future of leadership thinking will go, it is helpful to see the different bodies of opinion as a spectrum of current debate on the subject (see Table 6.1). At its simplest, this represents a range of views that have a heroic tendency toward the left and an anti-hero predisposition to the right. The debate on this is now getting into full flow.

TRANSFORMATIONAL LEADERSHIP

Toward one end of the spectrum is a body of thinking that sees the idealized leader as a transformer of businesses and organizations. While pedestrian leaders seek ways to achieve things – thus emphasizing the means over the ends – the transformational leader puts the ends (in the form of a goal or vision) above the means. Bernard Bass, professor emeritus at New York State University's school of management, is probably the leading exponent of this concept.

Such change leaders are needed, the argument runs, because they are the innovative, entrepreneurial transformers of tired, dispirited organizations. They visualize the form the new organization will have to take and then motivate people to make it a reality.

Such leaders are seen to have definable qualities. Typically they:

Table 6.1 Spectrum of current thought on leadership.

School of thought	Charismatic leadership	Transform- ational leadership	Adaptive leadership	Leader as builder	Learning leadership	Co-leadership	"Quiet" leadership	Leader- ship for greatness
Main ingredient	Inspirational charisma	Self- confidence and powerful vision	Fresh eye and fast reactions	Embeds organizational ability	Leaders released at all levels	Comple- mentary partnership	Thought- fulness rooted in experience	Humility and steely determin- ation 2001
Time-frame	Revived early 1980s	Mid-1980s	1990s	Mid-1990s	1990s	Late 1990s	Late 1990s	
Current status	Continuing research and promotion	Continuing research and promotion	Growing research and literature	Continuing influence	Diverse research continues	Needs more work and investigation	Beginnings of anti-hero movement	Brand new research

» see themselves as real change agents;
» are courageous and risk-taking, challenging conventional wisdom;
» believe in other people and their ability to achieve great things;
» are driven by their own powerful set of values;
» inspire those around them;
» handle ambiguity and uncertainty; and
» above all, they are visionaries.

Frequently quoted examples of transformational leaders include Lee Iacocca, who saved Chrysler in the 1980s, Lou Gerstner, who turned IBM around in the mid-1990s, and Steve Jobs, who returned to revitalize the company he founded, Apple, by the end of the 1990s. However, there are misgivings that this whole concept harks back too much to the "great man" idea that was discredited 50 years ago. And although there are psychological questionnaires designed to identify transformational leaders, skeptics argue that there is little empirical evidence that leaders thus identified go on to produce the successes expected of them.

THE CHARISMA ENIGMA

Further out along the spectrum are the so-called charismatic leaders.

The word "charisma" comes from the Greek word for "gift of grace" and has, through the ages, been used by the Christian church to signify a divinely bestowed power or talent. In the early twentieth century, German sociologist Max Weber identified charisma as one form of leadership authority – the authority bestowed on the leader by his or her followers (see Chapter 3).

In the mid-1970s, Robert House, currently professor of organizational studies at the University of Pennsylvania's Wharton School, began revisiting Weber's concept of charismatic leadership. Because "charismatics" have traditionally been associated with radical ideas – that change religions and societies – new life was given to the concept of charismatic leadership when US business suffered what was perceived as a leadership crisis in the 1980s. Radical reinvention was seen as vital to turn around America's corporate dinosaurs.

Charismatic leaders can, it is suggested, best be recognized by the reactions of their followers. For example, followers have deep faith in the leader's beliefs and/or vision and adapt their own beliefs accordingly. Their unquestioned acceptance of the leader means they become devoted to him or her and offer complete obedience. This means they develop an emotional attachment to the leader's goals and mission and seek to contribute to their successful achievement in any way they can. It is little wonder, therefore, that some in corporate America, with all its potential for hero-worship, saw salvation in finding such people.

The problems that can be caused by charismatic leadership have been repeatedly pointed out. One of the biggest flaws is the same one highlighted by Weber over 70 years ago – their powerful effect dissolves with the passing of the leader, leaving a void that is extremely difficult to fill. Such leaders are also prone to strong narcissistic tendencies that may prove dysfunctional for the enterprise and the people who work for it (see "The neurotic organization" below and "The dark side of leadership" in Chapter 8).

Many believe that charisma is a valuable, though not essential, asset in a leader. However, this is not a view shared by Peter Drucker: "The one and only personality trait the effective ones [leaders] I have encountered did have in common was something they did *not* have: they had little or no 'charisma' and little use either for the term or for what it signifies."[1]

Whatever skeptics may say about the hunt for the uniquely qualified leader who can assume the heroic role of savior, the transformational and charismatic schools (and others that metamorphose from them) will continue to have passionate adherents. The allure of the "great leader" remains strong.

ADAPTIVE LEADERSHIP

Take high-tech, global competition, industry convergence, the Internet, stir in any other familiar ingredients for a rapidly changing environment, and sprinkle liberally with elements of the "new" science – chaos and complexity – and you'll find a call for adaptive leadership. Leadership that enables an organization to *constantly* adjust and adapt to new realities – not just a one-off transformation. To keep it in this fluid state requires the ability to manage at "the edge of chaos" – the point between stasis and chaos where creativity, inventiveness, and corporate fitness can best be found.

Ronald Heifetz, co-director of the Center for Public Leadership at Harvard University and author of *Leadership Without Easy Answers*, believes that adaptive behavioral change is a challenge that traditional leadership simply cannot meet. To illustrate the scale of change that is required in some of today's business environments, he uses the example of gorillas. When threatened by a leopard, a group of gorillas will form a tight circle with the strong adult males on the outside of the ring, protecting the females and young in the center. This is a good defense against leopards, learned over thousands of years, but it is a bad response to modern poachers armed with guns and tranquillizer darts. To overcome this very different challenge requires entirely new ways of thinking – a quality that adaptive leaders need.

While a lot is being written about adaptive leadership, the key differences between the qualities required for this, as opposed to other forms of leadership, are not easily identified. Typically, high on the list is an ability to understand the complex business landscape and recognize – ahead of others – the non-linear changes occurring in it.

However, we should expect work on adaptive leadership – the ability to see with fresh eyes and react quickly in the right way – to continue and expand. A lot of research is going into complex adaptive systems (for example: our brains, immune systems, natural ecologies, even societies), so we can expect more ideas to be developed for managing complex behaviors and non-linear interactions.

LEADERS AS BUILDERS

At the start of the 1990s, Jim Collins, a management consultant and member of the faculty at Stanford University's Business School, and Jerry Porras, a professor of organizational behavior at Stanford, set out to establish the factors that underpin the "sustained corporate greatness" evident in companies like 3M, GE and Hewlett-Packard. In particular, they wanted to know what gives such companies their edge, so they compared each one with a close but less successful competitor.

In 1994, the results were published in *Built to Last: Successful Habits of Visionary Companies.* Translated into 13 languages, the book has since attained the status of business classic because its extensive historical research (a 70-year time-frame) enabled the authors to draw legitimate and often controversial conclusions.

At the heart of their findings is a powerful analogy: "Having a great idea or being a charismatic visionary leader is time-telling; building a company that can prosper far beyond the presence of any single leader and through multiple product life cycles is clock-building."

The authors' research shows that visionary, clock-building companies do not need either a great idea or a charismatic leader; indeed, it shows that the reverse is also probably true – really successful companies are best served by having neither. Charismatic leaders come and go, Collins and Porras argue, whereas long-lasting companies have the "organizational strength . . . to remain visionary and vibrant decade after decade." What matters is "the underlying processes and fundamental dynamics embedded in the organization" by the original, and successive, builder-leaders.

LEARNING LEADERSHIP

Around the middle of the spectrum, there are those who believe that the whole concept of the top leader is anachronistic, conjuring up as it does the "person who knows" and to whom others have to turn.

They propose instead a learning leadership in which the titular leader acts as mentor, supporter, facilitator, and teacher. Such leaders offer adroit guidance, smooth paths, generate communication, develop others, and, above all, listen. Rather than charismatically running the show, they leave real leadership to those throughout the organization who, at the micro level, explore new opportunities, lead positive change, challenge current perceptions, and, in the process, shape the business to more accurately fit its environment. Learning leadership everywhere.

Noel Tichy, professor of organizational behavior and human resource management at the University of Michigan's business school, argues that potential leaders exist at every level[2] – if only they can be spotted. So, as a corporate leader "your number one task is being a leader-teacher," someone who teaches, learns, and listens.

Debra Meyerson, a visiting professor at Stanford University, believes that organizations have plenty of "everyday leaders," whom she calls "tempered radicals"[3] – people who want to become valued and successful members of their organizations without compromising who they are and what they believe in. This means that as change agents they wrestle with how much they can rock the boat while still staying inside it. They are, in her view, crucial sources of new ideas and alternative perspectives, as well as providers of organizational learning and change. It is the top leader's role to discover these everyday leaders, tune in to what they say, see what differences they are making, find out what they are thinking, and provide the right support.

The "learning organization" has had a significant appeal ever since Peter Senge's book, *The Fifth Discipline*, proposed the concept in 1990. Since then, learning has entered the business lexicon and is increasingly attached to leadership qualities.

CO-LEADERSHIP

In one of his most recent books *Co-leaders: The Power of Great Partnerships*, co-authored with David Heenan, Warren Bennis has drawn attention to an under-investigated side of leadership – the way in which great leaders so often work with one (or more) close colleague. He cites as an example Steve Ballmer, Microsoft's president, who was responsible for launching the Windows™ operating system, hiring the company's pool of talent and much else that made Microsoft so successful. In his view, Ballmer has acted as the master tactician to Bill Gates' role as grand strategist – and thus the latter gets the superstar billing. The same retiring figure is, they suggest, present in many leadership situations.

Bennis believes that the very complexity of organizations today makes it practically impossible for one person alone to run an organization from the top. Co-leadership on the other hand "is a tough-minded strategy that will unleash the hidden talent in any enterprise. Above all, co-leadership is inclusive, not exclusive. It celebrates those who do the real work, not just a few charismatic, often isolated leaders, who are regally compensated for articulating the organization's vision.

"Today's celebrity CEO has become either a figurehead or an egomaniac, and often too public a personality to get the real work done. That work is done instead by teams of leaders – exceptional deputies who forge great partnerships to maximize both organizational and personal success."

Bennis and Heenan argue that the wise person defines success not in terms of personal fame but in what they achieve. In support, they quote the US Secretary of State under President Truman, George Marshal, who once said that there "was no limit to the amount good people could accomplish as long as they didn't care who received the credit. If you are concerned about the credit, you are paying too much attention to something other than the task."

This is an underdeveloped field and we can expect more work to follow.

LEADING QUIETLY

When Henry Mintzberg, professor of management at Canada's McGill University, gets close to a subject, you can expect sparks – or even fur – to fly. Ever since his reputation-building early work, *What Managers Really Do*, he has developed a taste for overturning accepted wisdom, attacking established theory, and challenging other expert opinion. You might expect that anyone who sees strategy as something to be crafted rather than drawn on a careful blueprint, who believes it emerges over time rather than falls out of a grand design, and who is therefore happy to head-butt Harvard Business School's strategy teachings, will have a view on leadership. And you won't be disappointed.

In this instance, Henry Mintzberg's acerbic words are directed at the US business press like *Business Week* and *Fortune*, as well as the so-called leadership gurus who, in his words, "personalize success and deify the leaders."[4] They talk of "Lou Gerstner's IBM," they ask headline questions like "AT&T: New Boss. New Strategy. Will it Work?" and "Can He [the new CEO] Fix Philips?" Mintzberg argues that this is a ludicrous over-simplification and perpetuates the myth that the white knight will ride in on his horse and fix it all. Except that, as he points out, "these knights mostly ride into territory they have never seen. (That's why they hire consultants)."

Change management is, in his view, the ultimate in managerial noise: "Companies being turned around left and right. All part of today's *managerial correctness*, which, in its mindlessness, puts political correctness to shame." Everything has to happen today – with 100 todays to turn a company round – and the new leader has to make a big, noisy impact.

Mintzberg suggests that what is really needed is a bit of "managing quietly." For him, quiet management is about thoughtfulness rooted in experience – a blend of wisdom, trust, dedication, and judgment (see Tesco example in Chapter 4). Such leadership is an integral part of the organization, has the respect of everyone there, and, because of this legitimacy, it actually works.

In a comment which strongly echoes Collins' and Porras' view on leaders as builders (see above), Mintzberg adds that "a healthy organization does not have to leap from one hero to another; it is a collective social system that naturally survives changes in leadership. If you want to judge the leader, look at the organization ten years later."

At a thought-leader conference, run by Harvard Business School Publishing in May, 2001, speakers such as Harvard's Rosabeth Moss Kanter and David Garvin took up Mintzberg's theme, stressing that, rather than being obsessed with larger-than-life leaders and grand strategies, there was a need for a quieter, more evolutionary approach to change.

We should expect the anti-hero movement to grow – it's probably time for the pendulum to swing.

LEADERSHIP WITH HUMILITY

Jim Collins has just completed another 5-year study that follows on from his work with Jerry Porras (see "Leaders as builders" above). This time he set out to find whether a good company could become a great company and, if so, how? The results of the research surprised both him and his team. Collins calls them counter-intuitive, and even counter-cultural,[5] for the US.

What they were looking for were companies that had performed at or below stock market values for 15 years, had a key transition point, and then had cumulative returns that outpaced the market by at least three times for the next 15 years. That is, good companies becoming, and staying, great. Having scoured the 1435 US companies that appeared in the *Fortune 500* between 1965 and 1995, they identified just 11 that met their criteria. For each of the 11 they then picked the best direct comparison company (by industry, size, etc.) and a further group of six companies that had short-lived moments of apparent greatness.

What they found was that the leaders at the critical transition point – and afterwards – had some unusual attributes. They were "modest and willful, shy and fearless." They were humble about their achievements, shunned public adulation, and were never boastful – attributing success to personal luck or excellent colleagues. They acted with quiet, calm determination and steely resolve, relying on high standards, "not inspiring charisma," to motivate people. They always took responsibility for any disappointments rather than blaming others or external events, and worked hard at finding successors who would build even more greatness into the business.

This, in Collins' view, is in direct contrast to leaders of the comparison companies. In more than two-thirds of these, the researchers came across what he describes as "a gargantuan ego that either contributed to the demise or continued mediocrity of the company." Among them was the much cited Lee Iacocca, feted for saving Chrysler from the brink of catastrophe and executing a brilliant turnaround. Collins thinks that, at least initially, this reputation was deserved – halfway through his chairmanship, Chrysler's shares were 2.9 times higher than the general market. But Iacocca then became self-absorbed, appearing regularly on television chat shows, personally starring in 80 Chrysler commercials, promoting his autobiography – which sold seven million copies worldwide – and thinking of running for president of the US. The result: "Iacocca's personal stock soared, but Chrysler's stock fell 31% below the market in the second half of his tenure." Clearly, it all depends which aspects of a charismatic or transformational leader you look at!

Collins' detailed quantitative and qualitative research adds weight to the end of the spectrum most antithetical to the charismatic hero. The impact will no doubt depend on the success of his book *Good to Great: Why Some Companies Make the Leap . . . and Others Don't*, published by HarperCollins in October, 2001. But it's already high on Amazon's sales list!

RECENT RESEARCH – BREAKING THE RULES

The largest leadership study yet undertaken is research into 8000 managers from over 400 companies, conducted by the Gallup Organization, to find what great leaders had in common. Marcus Buckingham and Curt Coffman published the results in their 1999 book called, interestingly, *First Break All the Rules*. So much, then, for all those prescriptive approaches.

It appears that great leaders do not have all that much in common – a finding that would come as no surprise to people like Warren Bennis and Peter Drucker. But it seems that the main rule they break is the way they handle people. They do not treat everyone the same, they specifically treat them differently.

Recognizing that each person has different skills, abilities, and motivations, they don't fall for the idea that with a bit more training everyone will be the same. They talent-spot and try to fit the right person into the right position, helping the best performers to perform better, rather than helping poorer performers improve. If they can't find the right niche for someone's unique talents, they don't hesitate to fire them.

In a nutshell, such leaders believe that people either don't or can't change – they can learn new skills and acquire fresh knowledge, but their fundamental nature will not change – so it's not worth trying to change it. Instead they try to tap an individual's talents – the behaviors and perceptive abilities that go with an individual's personality – or team them up with someone with complementary skills. Failing that, they can leave.

At one level, hence the book title, this looks like counter-intuitive stuff. At another level, it underlines one of the few commonalities in much of the thinking on leadership. Effective leaders appear to be people who do not need to pretend to be someone else; they are generally at peace with themselves, recognize their own strengths and weaknesses, and fit themselves into the right roles. They look for ways in which their natural talents can make the big difference. But they also replicate this process with others around them.

GLOBAL RESEARCH

Another large-scale piece of research currently underway is the 10-year Global Leadership and Organizational Behavior Effectiveness Research Project, with its suitable contrived acronym GLOBE.

Conceived in 1991 by Robert House of Wharton, it was funded in 1993 and now has around 170 social scientists or management academics doing research for it in over 60 countries/cultures around the world. Broadly intended to examine the interrelationships between societal culture, organizational culture, and organizational leadership, it is actually looking at what attributes of transformational/charismatic leadership (see above) are viewed universally as positive and negative and which vary according to culture (see "Multicultural leadership" in Chapter 5). Unfortunately, few of the findings are yet in the public domain.

However, Steve Hallam, dean of the University of Akron's business school, provides an early insight:

> "It is especially interesting to read about which leadership attributes are viewed very negatively in one culture and very positively in another. For example, in America risk-taking is viewed positively, but in many cultures American-style risk-taking is viewed as reckless. Leaders in some cultures are expected to be especially sensitive to subordinates' family problems, while in others it is viewed as meddling. A speaking voice that varies as to pitch and tone and expresses a wide range of emotion is seen by some to exhibit enthusiasm, but in others top leaders are expected to be above emotion and remain calm at all times speaking in a monotone. In many cultures being self-effacing is positive, but in others a leader is expected to behave in a more elitist manner."[6]

The final findings promise to be fascinating, even if they do focus on the charismatic/transformational leader.

IMPLICATIONS FOR INDIVIDUALS AND ORGANIZATIONS

The implications of these different views of leadership for individuals and organizations are many. Anyone in a working environment will have their own views of the leadership that they see about them. They will also be best placed to assess what alternative forms of leadership might work better. But it is unfortunate that the thinking on the subject tends to focus almost exclusively on what constitutes the best of leadership. So, all too often, the downsides of inappropriate or dysfunctional leadership are pushed to the sidelines. Among those who seek to redress the balance is Manfred Kets de Vries, a practicing psychoanalyst as well as professor of human resource management at INSEAD in France (see Chapter 8).

The neurotic organization

Kets de Vries, along with other psychoanalysts who work in the management field, such as anthropologist Michael Maccoby, point out that many corporate leaders are narcissists (see "The dark side of leadership" in Chapter 8 for more detail).

There are two types of narcissist – "constructive" narcissists are well-balanced and have a positive self-regard, and a secure sense of self-esteem. They also have a capacity for introspection, empathetic feelings, and an ability to "radiate a sense of positive vitality."

"Reactive" narcissists, on the other hand, are unbalanced, often driven by a "need to get even" and continually try to boost their defective sense of self-esteem. One of Kets de Vries' concerns is that being a reactive narcissist is not a barrier to success and that, if an unbalanced narcissist becomes leader, he or she is likely to create a neurotic organization.

Kets de Vries identifies the following five types of neurotic organization,[7] each reflecting the psychological condition of its leader.

» Dramatic – the leader craves attention, excitement, and stimulation. Reflecting this "strong leader" tendency, subordinates become dependent and only tell the leader what he or she wants to hear. Non-participative decision-taking means that self-aggrandizing action for action's sake (acquisitions, bold new deals) leads to impulsive and sometimes dangerously uninhibited ventures.

» Suspicious – the leader is hypersensitive, cold, distrustful, and acts as if some menacing force is out to get him or her. Power is centralized, information is constantly processed and analyzed, strategies are reactive. The culture emphasizes the power of information while distrust and intimidation walk hand-in-hand.

» Detached – the leader is withdrawn and may be indifferent to praise or criticism, showing neither warmth nor emotion. Strategy tends to be vacillating and inconsistent. Little flow of information or feedback from the leader provokes insecurity, conflicts, and inevitable jockeying for position.

» Depressive – the leader lacks self-confidence and self-esteem and may even fear success – so they often tolerate mediocrity. The organization is ritualistic, hierarchical, and resistant to change. Culturally, the leadership vacuum leads to lack of initiative, poor motivation, and negativity. Strategically there is a phobia about taking decisions.

» Compulsive – the leader needs mastery and control and so dominates the organization from top to bottom. He or she is dogmatic, obstinate, a perfectionist, and probably obsessed with detail, routine, and efficiency. Subordinates become submissive, uncreative, and insecure. The leader is likely to be obsessed with a single aspect of strategy, such as cost-cutting or quality, to the exclusion of all else.

People who succeed to leadership positions are not necessarily successful when they get there. Bad leaders can have seriously detrimental effects on the organization and the people within it. Those taking over neurotic organizations would do well to understand why they find things as they are.

KEY LEARNING POINTS

» There is a continuing interest in, and promotion of, charismatic, transformational leadership as an ideal – Bass, House.

» There has been a new emphasis on great insight and rapid response – adaptive leadership – Heifetz and others.

» The role of leaders as builders of a long-lasting enterprise, or the person able to make a good organization great, should not be overlooked – Collins and Porras.

» Learning, and leadership at all levels, enables the organization to shift and change to fit its environment on a continual basis – Senge, Tichy, Meyerson.

» In a highly complex environment, there can be a need to co-lead with someone who has complementary skills and abilities – Bennis.

» There are benefits in quietly getting on with the job without media fanfares – Mintzberg, Collins.

» There are dangers with dysfunctional leaders – Kets de Vries.

NOTES

1 Peter Drucker, *The Leader of the Future*, Jossey-Bass, 1996.

2 Noel Tichy and Eli Cohen, *The Leadership Engine: How Winning Companies Build Leaders at Every Level*, HarperCollins (paperback), 2000.

3 Debra Meyerson, *Tempered Radicals: How People Use Difference to Inspire Change at Work*, Harvard Business School Press, 2001.

4 Henry Mintzberg, "Managing Quietly," *Leader to Leader*, no. 12, spring, 1999.

5 Jim Collins, "Level 5 Leadership: The Triumph of Humility and Fierce Resolve," *Harvard Business Review*, January, 2001.

6 http://www.uakron.edu/cba/lead/tools.html

7 Manfred Kets de Vries, *The Leadership Mystique*, Financial Times Prentice Hall, 2001.

In Practice – Leadership Success Stories

What makes for effective leadership? Chapter 7 looks at three very different forms of successful leadership. It looks at, and draws lessons from:

» Jack Welch of GE – the legendary transformer;
» Akio Morita of Sony – the global visionary; and
» Archie Norman of Asda – the empowering leader.

"You can judge a leader by the size of the problem he tackles. Other people can cope with the waves, it's his job to watch the tide."

Antony Jay, author of Management and Machiavelli

JACK WELCH – THE LEGENDARY TRANSFORMER

Jack Welch, who retired as chairman and CEO of GE in September, 2001, after nearly 21 years in the post, is probably the most widely acclaimed example of an effective business leader in the world.

In the first half of the twentieth century, GE produced a string of innovative products, including the X-ray tube and the FM mode of transmission for radios. The company also extended its interests into a wide range of product areas, from national broadcasting to domestic electrical appliances.

During World War II, GE's revenues multiplied fourfold and by the 1960s GE competed in virtually every manufacturing industry, producing over 200,000 products, ranging from light bulbs to steam turbines. But its profit performance was poor. In the 1970s, although GE exited entirely from over 70 product areas, and earnings tripled, the company's share price performance remained mediocre. Investors, it appeared, believed that GE was too large and diverse to do anything other than track America's GDP in terms of performance.

On April 1, 1981, Jack Welch, then aged 45, took charge of what was the world's tenth largest industrial conglomerate at the time. He brought with him 20 years' experience in the business, having joined GE's plastics division in 1960 with a PhD in chemical engineering.

Ambition

From the outset, he made clear his ambitions. He told shareholders at his first annual general meeting that he wanted GE to be "a unique, high-spirited, entrepreneurial enterprise, a company known around the world for its unmatched level of excellence." Furthermore, he wanted it to be "the most profitable, highly diversified company on earth, with world quality leadership in every one of its product lines."

"My biggest challenge," said Welch, "will be to put enough money on the right gambles and to put no money on the wrong ones." Having watched two of his predecessors wrestle with an organization of GE's size and complexity, he decided to go for fast, dramatic change.

Restructuring

Welch set the new criteria. GE businesses would have to be either number one or two in their competitive global markets. Those that had no chance of achieving this were "to be fixed – sold – or closed." Welch then embarked on a huge program of restructuring, making $18bn worth of acquisitions and $9bn of disposals in the early 1980s.

Lean and agile

In parallel with this strategy, he was determined to create an organization that combined the speed and agility of a small company with the financial muscle of a large one. GE's existing management apparatus was, Welch avowed, a "ticket to the boneyard in the '90s."

First, he attacked GE's hierarchy by eliminating seven layers of mid-to-upper management and replacing them with two broad career-bands. In doing so, he reduced the layers of management between factory floor and executive HQ from nine to four.

He also "cleared out bureaucracy, along with the strategic planning apparatus, corporate staff empires, rituals, endless studies and briefings, and all the classic machinery that makes big companies smooth and predictable – but often glacially slow."[1]

"Neutron Jack"

Through this program of divestitures, restructuring, and downsizing, the company's headcount was slashed from 411,00 to 276,000. Welch was dubbed "the toughest boss in America" by *Fortune* magazine in 1984, but the nickname that stuck was "Neutron Jack" – because neutron bombs destroy people but not property. Opprobrium was heaped on him from all sides. Welch's response was to point out that everyone leaving GE had been treated with dignity and that the company "was doing 31% more volume with 31% less people." Savings were estimated at $6bn. Subsequently, Welch was candid about what he was doing – "I didn't have a morale problem. I created it!",[2] he told author Richard Pascale at the end of the 1980s, adding that "the leader who tries to move a large organization counter to what his followers perceive to be necessary has a very difficult time."

Speed, simplicity, and self-confidence

By the late 1980s, having tackled what Welch refers to as "the hardware" of the business, Welch embarked on the second stage of his plan. In his view, "most successful small companies possess three defining cultural traits: self-confidence, simplicity, and speed." So, under this banner, he switched the focus onto the human issues – "the software" of GE.

Rewards, roles, and responsibilities were made clear to each individual so that they could see a connection between their efforts and the company's success in the marketplace. The reward system was changed to encourage innovation, boldness, and risk-taking.

Welch wanted his people to be self-confident so that "their egos don't require that they originate every idea they use, or 'get credit' for every idea they generate." Self-confident people also don't need to use "business speak" or wrap everything in complexity – "self-confident leaders produce simple plans, speak simply, and propose big, clear targets." He wanted GE people to derive their sense of status from achievement, rather than position.

Empowering through "work-out"

At the end of the 1980s Welch also started a program of empowerment "with a difference." The program's name came from a hard question by a business school professor who had asked Welch: "Now that you have gotten so many people out of the organization, when are you going to get some work out?"[3] Welch liked the idea of "work-out" and turned it into "a relentless, endless company-wide search for a better way to do everything we do."

Welch was determined to ask the people who knew best how to run the company – employees – to develop solutions to important issues and also wanted their managers to make rapid decisions so staff could act on their ideas. In a typical work-out, groups of anything from 20 to 100 employees, representing a cross-section of position and function, meet off-site for two to three days to thrash out specific problems or seek new business solutions. Presentations are then given to senior management in the last half-day of the work-out. The senior managers have to decide then and there whether to approve or reject each idea on its business merits. The only other option is to ask for more information, in which case a deadline for decision-making is set.

As part of this initiative, GE's top business leaders also got together on a monthly basis to dismantle hierarchical and bureaucratic barriers to communication. Underlining his life-long hatred of bureaucracy, Welch declared time-wasting meetings and "the endless paper that flowed like lava from the upper levels of the company" as things of the past.

Boundaryless

Work-out was designed to empower all GE's employees and gain company-wide commitment to speed. But it was also intended to help Welch achieve his ambition of a "boundaryless" organization. Boundaryless, in his terms, is a type of behavior. It epitomizes the small company culture he wanted.

In particular, he wanted GE to be open to ideas, regardless of their source. He wanted to get people to look outside the traditional boundaries that restricted their thinking and narrowed their vision. Ideas should also "stand or fall on their merits – rather than on the altitude of their originators." The biggest reward Welch saw in being boundaryless was the end to GE's "not-invented-here" culture.

Values

By the early 1990s, Welch was defining the types of leaders who would succeed in GE. It was those who both delivered on commitments and shared GE's core values. Those who did not share such values would not last long.

Welch was as good as his word. Looking back in 1997, he was typically blunt. "In the early 1990s, after we had finished defining ourselves as a company of boundaryless people with a thirst for learning and a compulsion to share, it became unthinkable for any of us to tolerate – much less hire or promote – the tyrant, the turf defender, the autocrat, the big shot. They were simply yesterday."

Six Sigma

With increasing confidence that this new organizational climate and culture was now in place, Welch launched his next initiative, "Six Sigma," in 1995. Six Sigma, borrowed from Motorola and Allied Signal, was aimed at creating near-perfect quality in every process, product, and service within GE – moving from approximately 35,000 defects per million operations to fewer than four defects per million.

Quality would now be "the job of the leader, the job of the manager, the job of the employee – everyone's job is quality."[4] To reinforce this, he stipulated that, by January, 1998, nobody would be considered for any management job at GE, however junior, who hadn't been trained in Six Sigma and been involved in a successful quality initiative.

Digitization

At a meeting in March, 1999, Welch issued a challenge to GE's businesses. Called "destroyyourbusiness.com," the company's business leaders were set the task of reinventing their businesses for the Internet before a competitor did it for them. To reinforce the urgency and overcome fear of the Internet, 1000 of the company's top managers were paired with young, techno-savvy mentors to work with them three to four hours a week, using the Web, and learning to organize their computers, and their minds, for a future with the Internet.

In Jack Welch's words, this mentoring process "helped overcome the only real hurdle some of us had – fear of the unknown. Having overcome that fear, and experienced the transformational effects of e-business, we find that digitizing a company and developing e-business models is a lot easier – not harder – than we had ever imagined."

In 2000, GE sold $8bn of goods and services online – a figure expected to explode to $20bn in 2001. It now runs procurement auctions daily – expected to provide annual savings of $600mn by 2001. But the biggest impact has come from using the Internet for GE's internal processes. Welch expects this to take $1bn of costs out of GE's operations during 2001. "Old companies thought this was Nobel Prize-type work," Welch says. "This is not rocket science. It's just like breathing."

Teaching, but listening

Welch takes management education very seriously and regularly runs sessions at the company's Crotonville, New York training center. In an endeavor to free up people's risk-taking, Welch recounts his own worst mistake, the 1985 decision to buy Kidder-Peabody for $600mn – an acquisition that would ultimately cost GE some $1.2bn. The message is "if the boss can learn from his failures, so can you."

Welch also listens. In 1995 he was listening to members of a mid-level company training program who pointed out that the company's central tenet – to be number one or two in its markets – was losing it vital business. It transpired that business heads were narrowing their market definitions in order to achieve this positioning. Welch immediately ordered that in future they define their markets so that they had a market share 10% or less. As Welch acknowledges, "this simple but very big change, this punch in the nose, and our willingness to see it as 'the better idea,' was a major factor in our acceleration to double-digit revenue growth rates in the latter half of the '90s."

The result

At the time he left, in 2001, GE had seen 25% annual compound growth in its share price since he took over. Its market capitalization was $12bn in 1981 and is now $485bn – the largest in the world. Revenues of $27bn in 1981 grew to $129bn in 2000. Profit is up from $1.7bn to $12.7bn. Among many accolades, Welch was voted "Manager of the Century" by *Fortune* magazine. For four years in a row the same magazine has voted GE "The Most Admired Corporation in America," and the *Financial Times* has voted it "Most Admired Company in the World."

Little wonder, therefore, that most schools of thought on leadership claim him as an epitome of what they promote!

LEADERSHIP INSIGHTS – JACK WELCH

» Jack Welch's goal, from the beginning, was to create the entrepreneurialism, vitality, and fleetness of foot of a small company and marry it to the financial muscle that a large company can bring to bear.

» To change a giant of GE's size, Welch determined to shake it to its core right from the start. He risked the opprobrium and the dramatic drop in morale that followed because he wanted to clear the decks and create something he could grow. He believed that if you were third or fourth in a market you never really benefited in an upturn and suffered most in a downturn.

» Having dealt with the hardware, he then concentrated on the software. In wave after wave of initiatives, he clarified responsibilities, empowered everyone to come up with improvements, set high standards and values, and broke down barriers to the free flow of ideas. Only after he was quite sure that GE people were operating effectively did he start to drive big process changes – Six Sigma and digitization. There is a logical sequence to it all.

» Welch took action to change GE well before other US companies, largely because he foresaw the potential challenge of Japan. In consequence, the actions he took have become a role model for many other companies around the world. Welch has become an archetype.

GE time-line

» **1981**: Jack Welch takes over from Reginald Jones as chairman and CEO.

» **1981**: Welch declares all GE businesses must be number one or two in their sector.

» **1981**: Restructuring starts – over the next seven years 100,000 jobs are shed.

» **1984**: Welch dubbed "Neutron Jack," a title he hates.

» **1986**: Welch makes his own "worst mistake," buying Kidder-Peabody.

» **1988**: "Work-out" program starts.

» **1991**: GE begins to shed top and senior managers who don't adhere to GE values.

» **1995**: Six Sigma program introduced.
» **1999**: Destroyyourownbusiness.com and digitization initiatives.
» **2000**: Welch delays retirement to complete bid for Honeywell.
» **2001**: European Commission blocks Honeywell bid.
» **2001**: Jack Welch retires one year late.

AKIO MORITA – THE GLOBAL VISIONARY

When he died of pneumonia in 1999, Akio Morita, co-founder of Sony, was mourned around the world. The oldest son and fifteenth-generation heir to his family's 400-year-old sake brewing business, Morita would have been expected to take over the family legacy. But World War II and Japan's defeat changed all of that.

An end and a beginning

When naval lieutenant Morita first heard that an atomic bomb had been dropped on Hiroshima, he was staggered that the Americans had developed one so fast. And he knew the war was all but over.

In the aftermath of defeat, aged 25, Morita found a job as a teacher at the Tokyo Institute of Technology. But because, as a young boy, electrical appliances had always fascinated him, he also started to work part-time with Masaru Ibuka, a brilliant engineer with whom he had made friends during the war.

In 1946 Ibuka and Morita co-founded Tokyo Tsushin Kogyo KK, with an initial capital of around $500, and began working in a small room on the third floor of a bombed-out and abandoned department store in the center of Tokyo. The pair tried their hands at many things but eventually focused on producing a locally made tape recorder. However, when they finally succeeded, they could find no buyers.

Later Morita was to recall the significance of this experience: "I had never made anything for sale to anyone ... I had no experience in merchandising or salesmanship ... Ibuka believed strongly that all we had to do was make good products and orders would come. So did I. We both had a lesson to learn." It was one Morita would never forget.

Finding the breakthrough

Eventually, they found a strong market for their recorders in Japanese radio stations and schools and so, in 1952, Ibuka travelled to the US to see if there was a similar market there. He returned disappointed, but during his visit he talked with Bell Laboratories about licensing their new invention – the transistor.

The following year, with the Japanese economy still in a poor state, Morita knew they had to look at potential foreign markets if the company was to grow – and selling internationally had always been close to his heart. First, he went to the US to conclude the transistor licensing arrangement – an absolutely critical moment for the company. But otherwise Morita was discouraged – the US economy was booming and everyone seemed to have everything they could want. He had the same reaction in Germany, where post-war recovery had been much faster than in Japan. Only when he visited Philips in the Netherlands, and found that an internationally successful electrical giant could operate from an old-fashioned town like Eindhoven, did his courage return. "If Philips can do it, maybe we can, too," he wrote to Ibuka.

Breaking conventions

Back in Japan, Ibuka and his team set about developing a transistor radio – Bell Laboratories had warned them that the transistor's only commercial application was for hearing aids. Eventually they achieved their goal. Meanwhile, Morita's travelling experience had persuaded him that the name Tokyo Tsushin Kogyo was simply unworkable internationally.

Despite a great deal of internal opposition, he determined that the company's name would have to become much simpler and at the same time become a brand in itself. After months of thought, Morita and Ibuka eventually settled on a word that combined the Latin word for sound, *sonus*, and "sonny-boy" – American slang that was popular in Japan at the time. So Sony was born.

In a further break with tradition, Morita also decided that instead of a branding symbol – regarded as essential by Japanese companies at the time – the four letters of the name would be the brand. And, in spite of many reservations by the company's traditionalist advisers, the name was to be spelt in katakana, the Japanese alphabet used to write foreign names.

Courage

Thus prepared, in 1955, Morita returned to the US with a "pocket-sized" transistor radio, priced at $29.95, bearing the Sony brand name. Staying in cheap hotels, he tramped around electronics retailers in New York persuading them that big was not always beautiful. Amongst his meetings was the buyer from Bulova Co., who immediately said he wanted to order 100,000 of them. Morita knew that this order was worth several times the company's total capital, but the buyer insisted that the radios would have to carry the Bulova name. Despite being cabled by Ibuka and ordered by his board to accept the order, Morita decided to decline.

When Morita told him of this decision, the Bulova buyer exploded, pointing out that the Bulova brand had been built up over 50 years. Morita politely pointed out that Sony were therefore in the same place they had been 50 years before. "Fifty years from now I promise you our brand name will be just as famous as your company name is today," he said. Determined to build Sony into an international brand, Morita would later describe this as the best business decision he ever made.

Morita's perseverance paid off and he returned home with plenty of orders for the radio under the Sony brand. Although Sony's transistor radio was not the first in the world – a US company had produced one a few months earlier – it quickly became the leading make and, after success in the American market, it was not difficult to break into other international markets. From that point on Ibuka and Morita's confidence grew.

Breaking the rules

But Morita remained determined not to be trapped by the conventional wisdom found in other, generally much larger, Japanese companies at the time. Many of them were also exporting to the US, but used the big Japanese trading companies to handle distribution and sales. Morita decided that Sony would go direct and so he appointed an American agent.

But it wasn't easy. For instance, in February, 1960, Morita spent a freezing night helping four colleagues unload 30,000 transistor radios into a borrowed warehouse in downtown New York. However, later the same month, and despite much foot-dragging from the Japanese Finance Ministry, the Sony Corporation of America was incorporated with a capital of $500,000. Sixteen months later, Sony became the first Japanese company to offer its shares on the New York Stock Exchange.

Social networking

In 1963, although Sony Corporation of America was now up and running, Morita still believed that he had to know more about the American lifestyle. So, despite protests from Ibuka and his board, Morita moved himself and his entire family to New York. No Japanese company had ever had such a senior figure actually live abroad. For 16 months the family lived on Manhattan's Upper East Side. For his wife Yoshiko, who spoke no English, and their three young children, it was a difficult time.

Nevertheless this began Morita's long association with the US. His personal familiarity with the US markets enabled him to make important decisions – for example, that Sony's products would be high quality and premium-priced, not discounted. It also meant that the Morita family developed a strong social network.

As John Nathan, professor of Japanese cultural studies at the University of California, and author of a recent book on Sony[5] put it in *Time* magazine: "By the mid-'60s, though Morita was once again commuting from Tokyo, they had established a place for themselves in New York society, and Morita was on his way to becoming the best-connected Japanese businessman in the US." He was invited to join the international advisory boards of companies such as PanAm, IBM, and Morgan Guaranty Trust. In the process, he developed long-lasting personal relationships with many other US business leaders – something that would help Sony establish important and profitable joint ventures with companies like CBS, Texas Instruments, and Prudential Life Insurance during the 1970s and 1980s.

In 1970, as part of its global ambitions, Sony became the first Japanese firm to be formally listed on the New York Stock Exchange. Two years later, Sony became one of the very first Japanese companies to build a US factory.

Staying in front

Technologically, Sony also pushed ahead. Morita wrote in his 1986 autobiography *Made in Japan*: "The public does not know what is possible, but we do." In 1959 Sony announced the first transistorized television. It launched the Trinitron colour TV system in 1968 and led the way with home video, introducing its Betamax system in 1975. And, in 1979, the Sony Walkman was sprung on an unsuspecting world. Less well-known is its invention of the 3.5 in floppy disk, the world's first CD player, 8 mm video, and filmless camera – the Mavica.

Many of these developments were driven by Masaru Ibuka's passion for technology, but the two worked closely together – Morita in particular playing a significant role in the thinking behind the Sony Walkman. To Morita also fell the role of global marketeer, a part he played with consummate skill.

The achievement

In 1993, Akia Morita collapsed on a tennis court with a brain haemorrhage and thereafter effectively retired from work. Under his leadership, Sony had been instrumental in changing Japan's 1950s image as a maker of cheap, low-grade goods to that of a world leader in high-quality products across a spectrum of industries. In the process, he played a large part in turning his company into a multibillion-dollar enterprise. Among the scores of awards he received during his lifetime were the Légion d'Honneur from France and an honorary knighthood from the UK.

After his death, *The Washington Post* paid tribute to him as a man who had "helped create 'personal electronics', with products falling in price, weight, and size even as they rose in capability . . . Along the way, Mr. Morita's company . . . helped turn the words 'Made in Japan' into a symbol of unsurpassable quality."

But perhaps the sweetest accolade was a Harris poll, in 1998, which showed Sony had overtaken General Motors and General Electric as the brand name best known and most esteemed by US consumers.

LEADERSHIP INSIGHTS – AKIO MORITA

» Akio Morita knew that Sony had to be at the cutting edge of technology if it was to outpace Japan's existing and much larger electrical and electronics companies. But he learned his early marketing lesson well and applied it throughout his life.

» From an early stage he set the goal of turning Sony into a global brand. To achieve this he showed courage, commitment, and perseverance, coupled with astute judgment based on personal experience and knowledge. He also overturned conventional wisdom whenever it threatened to hinder the achievement of the goal.

» By living in the US, despite considerable inconvenience to his family and colleagues, he acquired a cultural affinity that stood the company in good stead. He also developed a personal and business network that played an important part in Sony's development.

» The long personal and working relationship with Masaru Ibuka is a classic case of co-leadership. Both brought quite different but complementary skills to their business and together took it to global leadership in its markets.

Sony time-line

» **1946**: Tokyo Tsushin Kogyo co-founded.
» **1954**: Sony brand name developed.
» **1955**: First sales of Sony transistor radios in the US.
» **1960**: Sony Corporation of America formed.
» **1963**: Akio Morita moves to New York for 16 months.
» **1968**: Sony UK formed.
» **1970**: Sony is first Japanese company listed on New York Stock Exchange.
» **1972**: Sony's first US factory built.
» **1993**: Akio Morita suffers stroke and effectively retires.
» **1997**: Masaru Ibuka dies.
» **1999**: Akio Morita dies.

ARCHIE NORMAN – THE EMPOWERING LEADER

Two Yorkshire farmers, Peter and Fred Asquith, with the backing of Associated Dairies, founded UK supermarket group Asda in 1965. After opening their first two stores, the company acquired two additional stores from a US company. One of these, in Nottingham, was huge for the time – over 7000 square meters of selling space – but rapidly became the most successful. From then on Asda would pursue a policy of building superstores.

The business expanded rapidly, concentrating on low prices and value for money, and over 20 years became one of the most successful retail companies in the country with 119 stores, mostly in the North of England. In the late 1980s, the company began to diversify, acquiring carpet and furniture retailers Allied Carpets and Maples. Then in 1989 it bought 60 stores from rival supermarket Gateway for £700mn – financed by borrowings.

Now burdened with debt, the company changed direction again, increasing its prices and chasing its leading competitors, Tesco and Sainsbury, upmarket. This proved to be a disastrous change of strategy and by 1990 the business had lost its way. Its 198 stores had a seriously demoralized workforce and the company itself had declining profits, rapidly rising debts, and a share price that was collapsing. Bankruptcy loomed.

Asda's board approached Archie Norman to take charge. A Harvard MBA, ex-McKinsey consultant and, at the time, finance director of Kingfisher – one of the UK's leading non-food retailers – Norman accepted the challenge.

First moves

When he met Asda's executive team for the first time, he made it clear that the business was in crisis and that rapid change was essential to save it. As he later recalled it, he set out the immediate steps he planned:[6]

» there were two fundamental objectives – securing the future of the business first and then creating shareholder value;

» the business would go back to its origins and core values – especially low prices and value for money. Beyond that, there could be no ''sacred cows'' and he had no magic solutions;

» work must start immediately on generating cash in every way possible, but he wanted two new experimental formats for Asda stores up-and-running inside 6 weeks;

» management would be reorganized to shorten lines of communication, create a focus on the stores, and build a united team. He wanted a culture that listened, learned, and responded quickly, based around common goals. He also wanted transparency, with everything being openly shared; and

» above all, everyone had to be close to the stores. ''We must love the stores to death; that is our business.''

He also warned them that his management style was forthright; he liked to argue and debate issues and expected both advice and disagreement. To underline that he meant to act swiftly, he fired Asda's finance director later the same day. Within a few days he announced a wages freeze – for managers and staff alike – and laid off all surplus employees.

Next steps

Taking advantage of his early ''honeymoon'' period as the new CEO, he strengthened the balance sheet by making a rights issue. Plans were made to sell the carpet and furniture businesses, something that was successfully completed in 1993. Simultaneously, he ordered a drastic reduction in prices to reassert Asda's position as the UK's lowest-priced national chain. By doing so, he halted the inroads being made by UK discount supermarkets such as Kwik Save, and stemmed the flow of customers to Tesco and Sainsbury.

Change from inside

Although he brought in consultants, it was only for short periods, and they were not there to define problems or draw up change programs. That, in his view, was management's role – Norman wanted his own people to manage change. But he was not confident that the original management, or many of the store managers, were up to the job.

A new team

In 1992, Norman brought in Allan Leighton as group marketing director. Leighton had worked at Mars for 17 years in a variety of management posts before becoming sales director of Pedigree Petfoods the previous year. Norman knew his strengths lay in strategy and knowing exactly how to position Asda to appeal to its customers. What he wanted was someone else to manage the change process with him. Allan Leighton's strengths were as a communicator and people manager – the ideal partner. The two men complemented one another perfectly and Leighton became Norman's right-hand man. Other changes were then made to the rest of the senior management group.

Objective and strategy

With a changed team at the top, Asda's mission was redefined "to be Britain's best value fresh food and clothing superstore by satisfying the weekly shopping needs of ordinary working people and their families who demand value." To deliver this, Norman wanted truly different formats from other supermarkets – a mix of fresh food, grocery, and clothing, as well as home, leisure, and entertainment goods – that was unmatched by other chains, and sales and service that had a distinct personality. The company already had a successful fashion line, unique to Asda, created by clothes designer George Davies. This would be rolled out to all stores as quickly as possible.

Breaking through

Although he and Leighton defined the overall direction, Norman was determined that Asda's employees had to be directly involved in the actual details of the changes. Individual store managers would have to lead change at the local level themselves, but he was not sure that many of them understood the scale of change he wanted.

So, he and Leighton decided to go over the managers' heads and engage employees direct. A well-publicized "Tell Archie" program was launched, designed to enable any employee, at any level, to come direct to him with new ideas or simply with their worries. He visited stores unannounced, wearing a badge saying "Hello I'm Archie" so that he could get feedback personally. At the same time, Leighton set out to create emotional commitment to the changes by winning everyone's participation. For example, Norman and Leighton formed a soccer team, in which they both played, and began a "Monday Night Football" competition for head office departments and the company's stores. The games were played at Leeds, and afterwards everyone - including Norman and Leighton - went out for pizza and beer together.

New formats

Cross-functional teams were put together to test new store formats with much flatter hierarchies. So successful were these stores that over the next six years virtually all stores were renewed or relocated - at a cost of nearly £1bn. Managers who could not cope with managing the change process in their own stores were dismissed, although many - used to highly centralized directives in the past - left voluntarily. Some financial rewards and incentives were used to keep the change process going, but Norman and Leighton placed more emphasis on winning commitment. They were concerned that too many measures attached to pre-planned goals could act as a barrier to much needed innovation and flexibility.

Equality and fun

To underline the transparency and egalitarian approach they wanted, no one in the Leeds headquarters had an office, with even Archie Norman's noticeably tidy desk sitting exposed to anyone who passed by. To blend fun with the commitment to change, anyone wanting to be undisturbed in the open plan offices put on a red baseball cap - which signified that they should be left in peace. Mondays became "black bag" days to encourage people to clear their desks, and the company became one of the first in the UK to introduce "dress-down Fridays," called "George" days to celebrate the company's popular fashion line. Conference rooms were named after fruit - Banana or Tomato Rooms - and there was a Big Table room, where a five-foot high table stood, with no chairs around it, to encourage meetings to be over quickly. Everyone was a "colleague," rather than an employee, and innovations were encouraged everywhere - for instance, store assistants began standing in the stores' parking lots with long poles and a flag that said "Parking

Space Here" to make life easier for drivers in a hurry. What worked was rapidly disseminated to other stores.

The achievement

Not only was Asda's decline reversed, but the company rapidly became one the UK's most admired retailers. Between 1993 and 1999 sales revenue grew from £4.9bn to £8.6bn, operating profits more than doubled from £190mn to £423mn, and its comparable store sales exceeded those of its competitors in every month over the period. One of the high street's most tired brands had been transformed into a real powerhouse that was suddenly nibbling at the heels of the two market leaders, Tesco and Sainsbury.

In 1999, a merger was agreed with Norman's old company King-fisher, but before it could be consummated US giant Walmart made a £6.7bn bid for Asda – valuing the company at 10 times more than it had been worth when Archie Norman took over. The offer was accepted.

LEADERSHIP INSIGHTS – ARCHIE NORMAN

» Archie Norman knew he had to move very fast to save Asda, but he stuck to making the big strategic decisions first. Strengthening the balance sheet, removing those who had got the business in trouble and, above all, taking it back to what it was good at. He avoided coming up with magic solutions.

» Knowing his own strengths and weaknesses, he brought in Allan Leighton and created a powerful partnership. Asda's staff "respected Archie, but loved Allan." Together they provide another example of successful co-leadership, built on the run.

» Having set broad direction, he then reached out and empowered employees throughout the company to help him make the changes that were needed. By empowering them, he made sure that those closest to the customer had the freedom to come up with ideas, but also the responsibility for the company's success.

» Throughout, he constantly set an example. He was approach-able, open, egalitarian, and injected fun into working life. Some of his ideas have been described as eccentric, but they worked.

Asda time-line

» **1965**: Asda founded.
» **1989**: 60 stores bought from Gateway for £700mn.
» **1990**: Prices in all stores raised.
» **1991**: Profit-warnings, share price collapses.
» **1991**: Archie Norman becomes CEO.
» **1992**: Allan Leighton joins; rights issue.
» **1993**: Allied Carpets and Maples sold.
» **1996**: Norman becomes chairman, Leighton takes over as CEO.
» **1999**: Wal-Mart acquires Asda for £6.7bn.

NOTES

1 Letter to shareholders, 1995.
2 Richard Pascale, *Managing on the Edge*, Simon & Schuster, 1990.
3 Albert Vicere and Robert Fulmer, *Leadership by Design*, Harvard Business School Press, 1998.
4 Janet Lowe, *Jack Welch Speaks*, John Wiley & Sons, 1998.
5 John Nathan, *Sony: The Private Life*, Houghton Mifflin Company, September 1999.
6 Michael Beer and Nitin Nohria (eds), *Breaking the Code of Change*, Harvard Business School Press, 2000.

Key Concepts and Thinkers

To understand many of the arguments about leadership, it's important to know some of the language. But it's also critical to know about important underlying concepts and why it can all go so wrong. Chapter 8 covers:

» a glossary;
» two key concepts;
» the dark side of leadership; and
» four key thinkers.

"Since 1900, there have been over 5000 studies on leadership, and there is still no comprehensive framework."
Philip Yetton and Jane Craig, Australian academics

Surprisingly, and unlike so many other management subjects, the broad area of "leadership" is *relatively* free of jargon. However, there are some terms that have their own particular meaning. What follows is a short glossary, a look at two of the subject's key underlying concepts, and a look at the important questions of how and why leadership can go wrong. The chapter concludes with details of a small selection of key thinkers.

GLOSSARY

Adaptive leadership – see Chapter 6.

Attributes – the qualities and characteristics of successful leaders. The list is endless, but typically includes: strength of character, charisma, courage, curiosity, decisiveness, energy, ethical values, integrity, intellectual capacity, intuition, judgment, resilience, and trustworthiness. A leader also has to be someone who has a powerful vision, is an excellent communicator, a good listener, an enabler, an example-setter, a motivator, and a priority setter. Clearly, only paragons need apply.

Charismatic leadership – see Chapter 6.

Co-leadership – see Chapter 6 and Chapter 7 for examples of co-leadership: Akio Morita and Masaru Ibuka at Sony and Archie Norman and Allan Leighton at Asda.

Cross-cultural leadership – the ability to lead in an increasingly global economy (for more, see "Multicultural leadership" in Chapter 5).

Empowering leadership – the form of leadership which is confident enough to push responsibility and decision-making out from the center to the parts of the organization that are directly in touch with customers (see the example of Archie Norman in Chapter 7).

Ethical leadership – an increasingly important area, not just from a moral perspective, but also because of the speed of communication and democratizing effect of the Internet. Organizations that fail to act ethically are increasingly prone to protest, demonstration, or boycott and not necessarily just in their home territory (see Chapter 5).

Heroic leadership – the style of leadership that some yearn for – the all-conquering hero who succeeds against all odds. It does occur from time to time, but invariably not where it is expected.

Leadership styles – the different styles and approaches that can be adopted according to the context in which leadership needs to be shown. See *Leadership Styles* in the *ExpressExec* series for the full background and detail.

Leading change – often seen as the biggest role for leaders in today's business environment (see "Transformational leadership" in Chapter 6).

Narcissistic leaders – see "The dark side of leadership" below.

Power – a critical element in leadership, since leaders normally hold some form of power over their followers whether it be the power of influence, persuasion, or control. So, while most leaders are, of necessity, power-wielders, the ones to beware of are the power-seekers–those who seek power for its own sake and then revel in its use. Leaders come in both forms. See "The dark side of leadership" below.

Servant leadership – a style of leadership first formulated by the late Robert Greenleaf in 1970. Sometimes hailed as the "grandfather" of the modern empowerment movement, Greenleaf described true leaders as those who lead by serving others – empowering them to reach their full potential. Although many expected interest in the subject to wane after his death in 1990, the reverse has been the case. See Chapters 6 and 7 in *Leadership Styles* in the *ExpressExec* series for more details and an example of servant leadership in action.

Situational leadership – an acknowledgment that the success or failure of leadership depends on the leader's ability to recognize and correctly interpret the situation in which his or her leadership will be displayed. See *Leadership Styles* in the *ExpressExec* series for more background and detail.

Spirituality in leadership – a growing area of interest, especially in the US where there is a perceived "crisis of meaning" in people's lives. The argument is that for many people work is now the central focus of their lives and therefore future leadership will have to find ways for people to fulfill themselves spiritually, not just socially and economically, at their work.

Transactional leadership – the concept that it is the transaction between the leader and the led (e.g., rewards, etc.) which provides the means for successful leadership. Transformational leadership puts goal-achievement above means.

Transformational leadership – see Chapter 6.

Value-driven leadership – leadership that takes a set of high-level values or principles as a central driver. Such values reflect the leader's own ideals, such as honesty, transparency, and openness, or caring, compassion, and consideration for others.

Visionary leadership – the essence of leadership is a clear vision – the goal or objective to be achieved or attained because without it there is nowhere to lead to. However, while vision may be necessary, it is rarely sufficient because other leadership abilities also have to be present.

TWO KEY CONCEPTS

Underpinning many leadership models are two fundamental concepts that date back to the 1960s. Because they are so deeply embedded, it is valuable to revisit them to understand their influence. Also included in this section are a number of concepts that help to explain the negative sides of leadership.

McGregor's "Theory X" and "Theory Y"

In 1960 Douglas McGregor, a pioneering psychologist in the field of industrial relations, put his finger on a key issue of leadership. He pointed out that "behind every management decision or action are assumptions about human nature." These assumptions, he proposed, could be categorized as "Theory X" or "Theory Y."

Those who assume that people are lazy, dislike work, and will avoid it if they can, believe in Theory X and therefore control, coerce, and punish people if they don't perform. Those who believe in Theory Y assume that people are quite prepared to work and give of their best if they have the chance and understand the need to motivate, create self-esteem, and instill a sense of achievement among their workforce.

To today's audience, Theory Y sounds much more attractive than Theory X. However, McGregor acknowledged that the right assumption may well depend on the situation – the nature of the workforce, the nature of the work – and saw nothing intrinsically wrong or bad about giving instructions or exercising authority. It is important to recognize that Theory Y underpins many of today's leadership approaches.

Maslow's "hierarchy of needs"

Abraham Maslow, the world-renowned psychologist, developed a "hierarchy of needs," first popularized in the 1960s. He divided them into two groups – "deficiency," or basic needs, and "growth" needs. The four basic needs were:

1 physiological needs – to overcome hunger, thirst, and have basic comforts;
2 safety or security needs – simply, to be out of danger;
3 "belonginess" and love – to be accepted, not to be lonely; and
4 esteem – to achieve, gain approval, and develop self-respect.

Once all of these needs are met – and only then – individuals set out on a path of personal development and growth. This also has four stages:

5 cognitive need – to know, to understand, and explore;
6 aesthetic need – to find symmetry, order, and recognize beauty;
7 "self-actualization" – to find self-fulfillment and realize one's full potential; to answer one's "calling" in life; and
8 "transcendence" – to help others find self-fulfillment and realize their own potential.

Maslow's basic tenet is that the more levels 7 and 8 are achieved, the more one develops wisdom and therefore knows what to do in a wide variety of situations. Effective leaders operate at these levels.

Yet the irony is that, just at the time that leaders are encouraging their employees to become empowered, to realize their talents, and fulfill their potential, today's competitive business environment may inhibit them from offering even the basic job security that lies at the deficiency end of the needs. Little wonder that trust has become such a critical issue in the leadership field.

THE DARK SIDE OF LEADERSHIP

Leadership can often go wrong. Here are four reasons why and how that can happen.

Leadership cults

Warren Bennis sums up the dangers of dysfunctional leadership in a few succinct sentences. "When cults develop around leaders, they begin to believe in their own infallibility, and anyone who believes that he or she can do no wrong is a menace. Idolatry turns people into lackeys, so mesmerized by their idol's talents that they neglect their own. Another problem with idolatry is that idols start believing their own press. They behave like mini-emperors, getting rid of dissenters or those who might have better ideas ... Far too often, these corporate potentates are empty suits, all sound and show, signifying nothing".[1] Psychologists explain the phenomenon in their own terms.

The wrong reasons

Manfred Kets de Vries points out that, because things can go wrong in childhood, children exposed to certain types of parenting may believe that they cannot rely on anybody's love or loyalty. As adults, such people remain deeply troubled by "a sense of deprivation, anger, and emptiness" and cope with this by turning their natural narcissistic tendencies into obsessions. Typically, such people become fixated by power, status, prestige, and superiority. So narcissism and leadership are intricately connected. "From many in-depth studies of leaders," Kets de Vries says, "I have concluded that a considerable percentage of them become what they are for negative reasons."[2]

Narcissistic leaders

Anthropologist and psychoanalyst Michael Maccoby has defined some of the weaknesses of narcissistic leaders.[3] Uncomfortable with their own emotions, they listen only to what they want to hear, seek to indoctrinate those around them, and dominate subordinates. Because they "are almost unimaginably thin-skinned," they cannot tolerate disagreement and dissent so they can be very abrasive with doubters or those who are brave enough to question them. They lack empathy, can be highly exploitative and are seriously competitive. Maccoby points to the title of the book written by Andy Grove, recent CEO of Intel, as a classic articulation of a narcissist's fear, distrust and aggression: *Only the Paranoid Survive.*

Power-seekers

Abraham Maslow believed that strong, tough people – the "power-seekers" and "power-wielders" – could become a force for either good or evil. Power-seekers in particular devote themselves to achieving power – often through an obsessive focus and by playing a "no-holds-barred" game.[4]

Because many people lack a strong sense of what they want, they are often ready to follow a self-confident leader. The problem is that, as Maslow puts it, "there is no more decisive-*looking* person in the world than a paranoid character. Also, there is no power-seeker more stubborn and persistent than the one who is paranoid."

This creates a situation in which people seek leaders who appear strong and unshakable in their beliefs, preferring them to more thoughtful, rational people who can see both sides of an argument. This plays directly into the hands of the "selfish, narcissistic, and power-driven people" who then use such followers as mere tools for their own advancement.

KEY THINKERS

Space prohibits reference to the scores of writers, academics, and psychologists who have contributed their own part to the massive jigsaw that makes up the current thinking on leadership (see Chapter 9). However, the following four thinkers are not only widely respected, but also represent four different approaches to the subject.

Warren Bennis

Warren Bennis has been referred to by *Forbes* magazine as the "dean of leadership gurus." He is Distinguished Professor of Business

Administration at the Marshall School of Business at the University of Southern California. He is also Visiting Professor of Leadership at the University of Exeter in the UK.

He has published over 900 articles in leading newspapers and magazines, and two of his books have earned the coveted McKinsey Award for the Best Book on Management. The *Financial Times* named his 1985 book *Leaders*, co-authored with Burt Nanus, as one of the top 50 business books of all time. His recent book of essays, *An Invented Life: Reflections on Leadership and Change*, was nominated for a Pulitzer Prize. In all, he has written more than 25 books, including the best-selling *Leaders* and *On Becoming a Leader*, both translated into 21 languages. Almost two million copies of his books are currently in print. Bennis has also received numerous awards and advised four US presidents on leadership issues.

Credited with reviving interest in the subject of leadership during the early 1980s, his writing has tended to become more populist as the subject has gained in popularity. However, he refreshingly acknowledges how little he still knows and understands about the subject. A reply to a recent interview question is typical: "The short answer is I don't really understand all that goes into developing leaders. If I had a recipe, I'd win the Nobel Prize."

He does, however, believe that there are a number of criteria for good leaders:

» business literacy and technical competence in the task at hand;
» people skills – especially the ability to understand, motivate, and communicate with them;
» conceptual abilities;
» a track record that merits a leadership role;
» the ability to select and grow the right people;
» judgment; and
» character.

The last two criteria are, he suggests, the reasons why top leaders often fail – poor judgment and weakness of character. And, tellingly, these are the most difficult (and may even be impossible) qualities to "teach."

Highlights

Books (many of these are also available on audio cassette):

» *Managing the Dream: Reflections on Leadership and Change*, Perseus Publishing, 2000 (previously *An Invented Life: Reflections on Leadership and Change*, Addison-Wesley, 1993).
» *Co-Leaders: The Power of Great Partnerships*, with David A. Heenan, John Wiley & Sons, 1999.
» *Leaders: Strategies for Taking Charge*, with Burt Nanus, 2nd edition, Harperbusiness, 1997.
» *On Becoming a Leader*, revised 2nd edition, Perseus, 1994.
» *Learning to Lead: A Workbook on Becoming a Leader*, with Joan Goldsmith, updated edition, Perseus, 1997.
» *Managing People is Like Herding Cats: Warren Bennis on Leadership*, reissue edition, Executive Excellence, 1997.
» *Why Leaders Can't Lead: The Unconscious Conspiracy*, reissue edition, Jossey-Bass, 1997.

John P. Kotter

John Kotter is Konosuke Matsushita Professor of Leadership at the Harvard Business School and is a renowned speaker on the twin topics of leadership and change.

Over the last two decades and more, he has written nine business books, a number of which have been best sellers, including *Leading Change* and *A Force for Change: How Leadership Differs from Management*. One of his most recent books, *Matsushita Leadership: Lessons From the 20th Century's Most Remarkable Entrepreneur*, won a *Financial Times* and Booz-Allen & Hamilton Global Business Book Award for Best Business Biography.

In his 1988 book, *The Leadership Factor*, he argued that, because of an emphasis on short-term results and lack of long-term vision, US companies were suffering from an acute shortage of the one quality required to win competitive advantage – leadership. In *A Force for Change: Leadership Differs from Management*, he returned to his contention that thousands of companies were over-managed and under-led, not for lack of leaders with charisma, but because so few really understood what leadership was and what it could achieve.

In fact, he argued that leadership was not about charismatic leaders achieving amazing results from their mere mortal followers, but lots of small acts of leadership achieved throughout the organization, running alongside good everyday management.

Some people find Kotter's work highly prescriptive, for instance, in *Leading Change* he asserts that there are just eight steps to take – no more and no less. But this goes for many books in the leadership genre.

Highlights

Books:

» *What Leaders Really Do*, Harvard Business School Press, 1999.
» *Matsushita Leadership: Lessons From the 20th Century's Most Remarkable Entrepreneur*, Free Press, 1997.
» *Leading Change*, Harvard Business School Press, 1996.
» *A Force for Change: Leadership Differs from Management*, Free Press, 1990.
» *The Leadership Factor*, Free Press, 1988.
» *The General Managers*, MacMillan Publishing, 1986.
» *Power and Influence/Beyond Formal Authority*, Free Press, 1985.

Articles:

» "Leading Change: Why Transformation Efforts Fail," *Harvard Business Review*, March–April, 1995.
» "What Leaders Really Do," *Harvard Business Review*, May–June, 1990.

Further information:

» http://dor.hbs.edu/fi_redirect.jhtml?facInfo=bio&facEmId=jkotter
» http://www.eitforum.com/Experts/john_kotter.htm

Manfred Kets de Vries

Manfred Kets de Vries is Professor of Human Resource Management at INSEAD in France, and an independent consultant. His area of expertise and research is the interface between psychoanalysis/dynamic psychiatry and management, especially in the areas of leadership and the process of organizational transformation and change.

Prior to joining the faculty at INSEAD, Kets de Vries practiced as a psychoanalyst and taught at McGill University and the École des Hautes Études Commerciales, both in Canada, as well as Harvard Business School. He was awarded The Critics Choice Award for the most acclaimed business book of 1995: *Life and Death in the Executive Fast Lane*. He is the author of 11 books and over 100 scientific papers.

Kets de Vries has been listed by the *Financial Times*, *Wirtschaftswoche*, *Le Capital*, and *The Economist* as one of Europe's business gurus. His work on leadership is particularly significant because he provides an invaluable balance to those who see and write about only the positive sides of leadership. Kets de Vries is not afraid to look hard at the potential damage that psychologically unstable leaders can have on organizations (see "The neurotic organization" in Chapter 6 and "The dark side of leadership" earlier in this chapter).

Highlights

Books (many are available in foreign language editions):

» *The Leadership Mystique: A User's Manual for the Human Enterprise*, Financial Times Prentice Hall, 2001.
» *The New Global Leaders*, Jossey-Bass, 1999.
» *Life and Death in the Executive Fast Lane: Essays on Organizations and Leadership*, Jossey-Bass, 1995.
» *Leaders, Fools and Impostors: Essays on the Psychology of Leadership*, Jossey-Bass, 1993.
» *Organizations on the Couch*, Jossey-Bass, 1991.
» *Prisoners of Leadership*, John Wiley & Sons, 1989.
» *The Neurotic Organization: Diagnosis and Changing Counter-Productive Styles of Management*, with Danny Miller, Jossey-Bass, 1984.

Further information:
http://www.insead.edu/~vries/fullcv.htm

John Adair

John Adair is known internationally as a writer, teacher, and management consultant on the subject of leadership. After a colorful early career, he became Senior Lecturer in Military History and Advisor in Leadership Training at the Royal Military Academy, Sandhurst, England. He was appointed as the world's first Professor of Leadership Studies at Surrey University in 1978, and is currently Visiting Professor of Leadership Studies at the University of Exeter. He is the author of 26 books.

Adair has been a consistent exponent of the way in which leadership skills can be developed, believing it to be a transferable skill rather than an inborn quality. He pioneered the Action-Centred Leadership (ACL) model while teaching at Sandhurst. This consists of three overlapping circles: achieving the task, building and maintaining the team, and developing the individual (for more details see *Leadership Styles* in the *ExpressExec* series). Adair believes ACL to be a universal approach that works across different cultures. It is estimated that over two million people worldwide have participated in ACL training.

Highlights

Books:

» *John Adair's 100 Greatest Ideas for Effective Leadership and Management*, Capstone, 2001.
» *The John Adair Handbook of Management and Leadership*, Hawksmere Ltd, 1998.
» *Not Bosses but Leaders: How to Lead the Way to Success*, Kogan Page, revised edition, 1990.
» *Great Leaders*, Talbot Adair Press, 1989.
» *The Action-Centred Leader*, Industrial Society, 1989.

NOTES

1 http://westy.jtwn.k12.pa.us/users/sja/Bennis.html
2 Manfred Kets de Vries, "The Leadership Mystique," *Academy of Management Executive*, vol. 8, no. 3, 1994.
3 Michael Maccoby, "Narcissistic Leaders: the Incredible Pros, the Inevitable Cons," *Harvard Business Review*, Jan–Feb, 2000.
4 "Leaders, Pawns and Power," *The Maslow Business Reader*, edited by Deborah C. Stephens, John Wiley & Sons Inc., 2000.

Resources

Thousands of studies and books have been produced on leadership. Chapter 9 looks at some of the better sources and resources for those who want to know more (with Websites where appropriate):

» foundations, centers, and institutes;
» journals and magazines; and
» books on different aspects of the subject.

"Leadership has been the subject of an extraordinary amount of dogmatically stated nonsense."

Chester Barnard, businessman and author

Anyone looking for information on leadership will find him or herself confronted by an astonishing array of sources and resources. For example, entering "leadership" in Google's search engine (www.google.com) will produce over six million results.

The problem is that there are so many different areas where leadership is applied, so you'll find specialist material on leadership in education, communities, nursing, politics, and school administration as well as for student leaders. Looking for the obvious names can also feel misleading. For example *the* Leadership University is sponsored by Christian ministries, and *the* Leadership Institute turns out to be a resource for grass root conservative activists in the US.

There are also so many leadership programs in the US that there is a central clearing-house for leadership materials and resources based at the University of Maryland. And, of course, there is a plethora of white papers produced by consultants and many newsletters – for example, those published by the Leadership Institutes at American universities, many of which have their own leadership "journals."

However, the following have been picked out as some of the most useful resources for anyone wanting more information on corporate and business leadership.

THE PETER F. DRUCKER FOUNDATION

http://www.pfdf.org

Although this foundation is primarily intended for non-profit management, it is a prime resource for anyone interested in leadership – not least because it publishes a quarterly journal *Leader to Leader*, with articles written by leaders from both academic and business communities as well as respected social thinkers. It also runs conferences on leadership subjects, and offers videos and online "Drucker" courses.

On its Website, there is an invaluable thought-leaders' forum, providing profiles and contact details for over 250 leading management thinkers. But that is only the beginning, because it also offers extracts from relevant books and, most importantly, all articles previously published in *Leader to Leader* are freely available – back to 1996 (see http://www.pfdf.org/leaderbooks/l2l/index.html).

Here you will find articles by Warren Bennis, Peter Senge, Charles Handy, Noel Tichy, John Kotter, Max de Pree, Henry Mintzberg, and many more.

LEADERSHIP CENTERS AND TRUSTS

Many countries have trusts, foundations, and centers devoted to leadership. The ones listed here are therefore only a sample of those that can be found.

Ohio State University

http://www.ag.ohio-state.edu/~leaders/

As you might expect, Ohio State University (see Chapter 3) has its own Leadership Center although, surprisingly, it only started in 1990. It has a quarterly publication called *Leadership Link*, started in 1996, which is offered both in printed form and online (though you'll need Adobe Acrobat Reader to view it). You can also subscribe to their weekly e-mail *Leadership Moments* (very short, one-page thought-provokers) or *Leadership Discoveries*, which comes out monthly and is slightly longer.

University of Southern California

http://www.marshall.usc.edu/main/magazine/institute.cfm

Warren Bennis is the founder and chairman of The Leadership Institute at USC's Marshall School of Business. It was started in 1991 to address the "critical need for new leadership." The Institute's activities cover three areas: research; leadership development programs for the university; and conferences. There are no resources online.

State University of New York

http://cls.binghamton.edu/

Bernard Bass (see Chapter 6) is involved in Binghamton University's Center for Leadership Studies at the State University of New York. Founded in 1987, it conducts research to discover and verify new knowledge about a full range of leadership potential – though, given Bass's interest in transformational leadership, it is no surprise to find this topic prominent. Although its Website provides lists of articles, research reports, and manuscripts, sadly the center seems to be otherwise quiescent – with no other online offerings. Maybe this is because the papers from the Kellogg Leadership Studies that began at Binghamton are now available at the James MacGregor Burns Academy of Leadership (see below).

Wharton School

http://leadership.wharton.upenn.edu/welcome/index.shtml

Robert House (see Chapter 6) is a professor at the University of Pennsylvania's Business School, which has a Center for Leadership and Change Management. The center has published a monthly *Leadership Digest* since 1996, and all articles from all issues are available online at no cost.

Stockholm School of Economics

http://www.caslnet.org/

The Centre for Advanced Studies in Leadership (CASL) is located at the School of Economics but is a collaborative venture between the school, Sweden's Royal Institute of Technology, and the Swedish National Institute for Working Life. It organizes seminars, workshops, courses, and conferences in the field of leadership and promotes interdisciplinary research. Details of current projects as well as full research papers, some articles and book extracts (all requiring Adobe Acrobat Reader) are available under "research" on their Website. CASL also publishes a leadership journal, *Ledmotiv*, three times a year.

University of Maryland

http://www.academy.umd.edu/home/index.htm

Housed at the university is the James MacGregor Burns Academy of Leadership. Its span is much wider than business leadership, using education and training to foster principled leadership, especially for "groups historically under-represented in public life." It is a think-tank, training center, and educational institution all rolled into one.

There is a wealth of papers and articles available on the Website (under "publications"), including the Kellogg Leadership Studies Project Working Papers (see above).

Leadership Trust Foundation

http://www.leadership.org.uk/

A UK foundation, based in Ross-on-Wye in Herefordshire. Its overall mission is to enhance and influence leadership and leadership development in all aspects of society, throughout the UK and Europe. It has a Research Centre for Leadership Studies, an Innovation and Development Department, and offers an MBA with a specialism in leadership in conjunction with Strathclyde University's Business School.

JOURNALS

Remarkably, there are no journals that concentrate exclusively on leadership – many contain the word in their title, but they cover a huge range of subjects that are only tangentially related. You can stretch leadership as wide as you like.

There are, however, a number of management journals which do carry significant articles that add to the leadership debate and a selection is considered below.

Harvard Business Review

http://www.hbsp.harvard.edu/home.html

Internationally known, *HBR* has carried many articles on leadership over its 79-year history – not least because an *HBR* article is a good launch pad for a future book. Published bi-monthly until recently, it is now a monthly publication.

Its publishing company, Harvard Business School Publishing, is also a large-scale management and business book publisher, so as a combined resource their Website is worthwhile visiting. At present, by selecting the topic "leadership," there are nearly 900 products available, while leadership and its sub-topics combined have over 1500 products. But note, they are only for sale.

You also need to be aware that it is easy to be confused by what is a "faculty sample," a "library set," an "Onpoint" edition, etc. The terminology is not customer-friendly and you can easily spend more than you intended. Nevertheless, you can get access to important, downloadable *HBR* articles if you know what you are looking for and persevere – the cost is minimal.

Sloan Management Review

http://mitsloan.mit.edu/smr/

A publication from the Sloan School of Management at the Massachusetts Institute of Technology (MIT). Here, a search for leadership on their own homepage yields 60 responses, asking the same question at MIT's site provides 84. And the "abstract" of each article, in both cases, is non-existent. However, there are some good articles to buy if you know what you want.

California Management Review

http://www.haas.berkeley.edu/News/cmr/index_.html

Now celebrating its 44th year of publication, *California Management Review* comes out of the Haas School of Business at the University of California at Berkeley. Although it publishes some good articles – including some by Warren Bennis – its search facilities are pathetic. You can get hold of a "complete" or "descriptive" index but you have to wade through them or know what you are looking for.

European journals

http://www.elsevier.nl/homepage/alert/?mode=direct

There are two general publications that carry some articles on leadership: *European Management Journal* and *Long Range Planning*. Both are owned by Reed Elsevier and carry the Pergamon imprint from Elsevier Science. Unfortunately, unless you subscribe you have to go through logins with username and password even to check journal content. If you persevere you will find some articles of value. Elsevier is making money out of its online offerings and keeps it that way.

MAGAZINES

Most countries have management or business magazines that provide profiles of business leaders, though many are thinly disguised PR opportunities.

There are also a number that have international or European editions, such as *Business Week*. The one that particularly receives Henry Mintzberg's ire (see Chapter 6) is *Fortune* magazine, a bi-weekly that heavily associates individual leaders with their organizations' success or failure. See www.fortune.com.

BOOKS

There are thousands of books that focus on, or purport to be about, leadership. Punch in "leadership" at amazon.com and you'll get over 10,000 matches! So here is a selection, inevitably arbitrary, to add to those already specifically mentioned in earlier chapters.

Collected works

If you like many different viewpoints within a single book, the collections of essays are for you. Here are two good examples.

» *The Leader of The Future*, published by the Peter F. Drucker Foundation (see above) in 1996 – this book has a collection of essays by selected thought-leaders. It includes the thinking of Peter Senge, Charles Handy, Ed Schein, Dave Ulrich (see Chapter 2), and Rosabeth Moss Kanter, among many others. You won't be able to agree with what everyone is saying, but you'll certainly get some different perspectives.

» *The Future of Leadership*, published in 2001 by Jossey-Bass (John Wiley & Son) – this collection of essays includes Warren Bennis among its editors. Contributors include Bennis himself, Edward Lawler, Charles Handy (again), Thomas Davenport, Tom Peters, James Kouzes, and Barry Posner.

Role models

There are many books that seek to offer leadership role models, not least the autobiographies of "leaders" themselves – Lee Iacocca's memoirs were a world best-seller (see Chapter 6).

But the following two books provide not only an insight into leaders and the way they lead, but also provide cultural and global dimensions.

» *The New Global Leaders*, by Manfred Kets de Vries, published by Jossey-Bass in 1999 – this book enables Kets de Vries to identify what he perceives as the attributes that global leaders need, by telling the contrasting stories of Richard Branson of Virgin, Percy Barnevik of ABB and David Simon of BP.
» *21 Leaders for the 21st Century*, by Fons Trompenaars and Charles Hampden-Turner, published by Capstone in 2001 – this book lets Trompenaars and Hampden-Turner (see Chapter 5) describe and develop their concept of "transcultural competence." In it, they interview and recount the story of 21 leaders, including Philippe Bourguignon of Club Med, Christian Majgaard of Lego, Edgar Bronfman of Seagrams, and Charles Moody-Stuart of Shell. All those included in the book are, or have been, leaders of internationally known companies.

Heavyweight

Reference

If you want to dig deep into the subject, you can always attack Bernard Bass and Ralph Stogdill's *Handbook of Leadership: Theory, Research, and Managerial Applications* (see Chapter 2). Now in its third edition (published in 1990), it is a powerful reference for the serious student of the subject. But, at 1182 pages, you probably need to be serious and, of course, its content is dating because it omits the last 10 years' developments.

Probably it would be better to go for *Leadership in Organizations* by Gary Yukl, published by Prentice Hall's College Division. Its fifth edition came out in 2001, and it runs to only 600 pages – but covers the main theories and research on the subject.

Particular themes

Transformational leadership

Probably the best resource here is *Improving Organizational Effectiveness Through Transformational Leadership*, by Bernard Bass and his close colleague Bruce Avolio. It was republished as a paperback in 1993 by Sage Publications.

Charismatic leadership

Try *Charismatic Leadership: The Elusive Factor in Organizational Effectiveness*, written by Jay Conger and Rabindra Kanungo. Originally published in 1988, it has recently been reissued in paperback. Conger is chairman of the Leadership Institute at the University of Southern California and charismatic leaders studied in the book include Ross Perot, Lee Iacocca, and Steve Jobs.

Adaptive leadership

Although there is much more to this book than adaptive leadership, *Leadership Without Easy Answers* by Ronald A. Heifetz, is to be strongly recommended. Published in 1994 by Belknap, don't expect an easy read, but as professor at the John F. Kennedy School of Government, Heifetz has much to say about power, its roots, and the importance of values in leadership. It's a book to get you thinking.

Learning leadership

There are many books that touch on this area. One to try is *The Leadership Engine: How Winning Companies Build Leaders at Every Level*, by Noel M. Tichy and co-writer Eli Cohen – Tichy is someone who has been a long-term close observer of GE. Also, Deborah Meyerson's new book, published in 2001, *Tempered Radicals: How People Use Difference to Inspire Change at Work*, contains interesting ideas about "everyday" leaders (see Chapter 6).

Learning to lead

Many books refer to their author's belief that leaders are made not born and that leadership can be learned, but few give a route map to the process. One that does is *The Leadership Challenge: How to Keep Getting Extraordinary Things Done in Organizations*, by James Kouzes and Barry Posner. Reprinted as a second edition by Jossey-Bass in 1996, it had a 35,000 first print-run.

Spirituality in leadership

The growing interest in the US in spirituality, as a way to create a value-driven, ethical organization that provides more than just a monthly pay check, was mentioned in Chapter 8. If this interests you, see *Spirit at Work: Discovering the Spirituality in Leadership*, in the Jossey-Bass Management Series, edited by Jay Conger and published in 1994. Or the more recent *Capturing the Heart of Leadership: Spirituality and Community in the New American Workplace*, by Gilbert Fairholm, from Praeger Publishing in 1997.

Overall

A recently published book that is highly recommended is *The Leadership Mystique: a user's guide for the human enterprise*, by Manfred Kets de Vries. Published in 2001, it covers emotional intelligence, effective leadership, the roots of failure, global leadership, and many other subjects that are critical to the subject. Clearly written, it is full of good self-check questions (as opposed to the often awful ones found in other books). "Organizations," in Kets de Vries' view, "are like automobiles. They don't run themselves, except downhill." For a big view of leadership, this book, from one of Europe's best management thinkers, is a good place to start.

Meanwhile, elsewhere ...

If you want to track down a book on leadership by finding the publisher, or browse through the titles and authors, then try Australia's Melbourne Business School McLennan Library Website on the subject: http://www.mbs.edu/library/mconline/bibliographies/Pdf/Leadership. pdf. You'll need Adobe Acrobat Reader, but it's well worth having on file.

Or, if you want to cheat and look at quotations and excerpts of Warren Bennis and Burt Nanus' writings, there is an astonishing Website offered by Westmont Hilltop School District in Pennsylvania. Go to http://westy.jtwn.k12.pa.us/users/sja/ and look at the lower half of the page. You can also catch up on Attila the Hun!

Alternatively, for light relief, why not try http://www.leadersdirect. com/leadership.html, a UK Website that gives lots of one-line ideas and thoughts on leadership.

Ten Steps to Making Leadership Work

There is no formula for successful leadership, but there are areas which are important and will improve the likelihood of success. Chapter 10 looks at what existing, about-to-be, or aspiring leaders should consider, including:

» know yourself;
» and go on learning;
» don't assume anything;
» have clear objectives;
» be decisive;
» choose the right people;
» devolve power;
» lead by example;
» act with integrity; and
» know when to go.

"Good judgment is usually the result of experience. And experience is usually the result of bad judgment."

Robert Lovett, US Secretary of Defense (1951–3)

Leadership proves to be extremely difficult to define, a result of the elusive qualities it can contain. Even what makes for successful leadership is the subject of many, often conflicting, theories. Yet around the globe, in hundreds of thousands of different situations, people are expected to show it.

What, then, can they do to meet these expectations? How can they put this art or process to work? For those who are already in leadership positions, what "sanity check" can they run on their effectiveness? For those about to shoulder the mantle, what are the key things to think about? For those who aspire, what preparations can they be making?

Perhaps the first thing to be said is that worrying about personal attributes, traits, or characteristics is low on the list. Both Peter Drucker and Warren Bennis are agreed that the effective leaders they have met and known come in all shapes and sizes, colours, and creeds. Bald, fat, tall, and thin. For everyone who argues that charisma is essential, there are those who argue that it is irrelevant. For everyone who argues that overt self-confidence is crucial, there are those who can point to successful leaders who showed modesty and humility.

Perhaps no clearer example exists than two successive British prime ministers. In 1945, Winston Churchill, the epitome of a charismatic, pugnaciously self-confident war-leader, was replaced by a retiring, modest politician called Clement Attlee – someone of whom Churchill witheringly once said: "He's got plenty to be modest about." Yet in two different situations these leaders were astonishingly successful – Churchill in holding Britain steadfast and then building and sustaining an alliance that would achieve victory in World War II, Attlee in introducing a range of welfare and social reforms that underpin British society today.

So what does matter? Of course, there is a myriad of things. If there were a formula, then, as Bennis said, he'd have won a Nobel Prize with it. But by filtering the literature carefully it is possible to come up with 10 things that are important. They won't, of themselves, make anyone a leader, but they will improve leadership if and when the time comes. Here they are.

1. KNOW YOURSELF

The prime imperative on which almost all leadership authorities agree is to know oneself. Part of this is to know what one is good at - how one excels. It is such strengths that any good leader will play to. Nobody is good at everything, however much they may want to be. Knowing how to undertake the task involved is important, but knowing where one can make the greatest difference is critical.

But that is only half the equation. Recognizing one's weaknesses is the other. This can be difficult because many people develop a blind spot about their own failings, but it is essential not just to know what they are, but also to understand how to mitigate their effect. Good leaders know a lot about themselves through a process of self-reflection. They don't see this as time wasted, because they gain considerable inner strength from doing it. Knowing yourself, after all, reduces the likelihood of surprising oneself - especially in a negative sense. There are plenty of unwanted surprises that come from other sources.

Self-awareness also opens minds to how other people may be feeling or thinking, or why they are reacting in the way they are. It can help to create "mindfulness."

2. AND GO ON LEARNING

Successful leaders never stop learning - from successes, from mistakes, from experience, from what they see happening around them. They learn from their competitors, partners, customers, colleagues, and often from those completely unconnected with their particular industry or business area.

The truism that "the older you get, the more you know how much you don't know" is not a comment about senile decline, but a warning against the belief that anyone can know all they ever need to know. Lifelong learning has become a somewhat hackneyed phrase, but in today's fast-moving business environment it is an essential - particularly for a leader.

Part of learning is also the need to unlearn, to get rid of beliefs and assumptions created in the past that no longer apply. Many leaders make the mistake of transferring experience drawn from one situation directly into a very different situation, usually with unfortunate results.

Chapters 4 and 5 looked at the implications of new technologies and a globalizing economy. In a very practical sense, these provide examples of just how much learning is necessary - for instance, to stay at the cutting edge of what technology can offer - and how much unlearning may be needed, to avoid cultural stereotyping and our continuing propensity to act "mindlessly."

3. DON'T ASSUME ANYTHING

Effective leaders have, or acquire, an ability to probe and question. They do not take things at face value and never assume anything. Good leaders are curious, they frequently ask "why?" Many develop an uncanny ability to ask *the* searching question that uncovers a fudge, an oversight, or a misjudgment.

While this is often a reflection of intelligence or personal insight, it is just as often a result of intent listening, of situational awareness and considered thought. Not for such leaders the hectoring questions and bullying performance, instead they focus their attention so well that they can see the disconnections, the inconsistencies, or the incongruities. Such skills can be learned.

In a frenetic world, it is easy to slip into seeing business as a series of problems to be solved. This frequently leads to the problem-solving approach to management so beloved by consultants. Instead of hurrying to fix things that are broken, good leaders try to find out why things aren't working in the first place. They look below the superficial problem and try to find the underlying issues, because until these are resolved, problems will keep recurring. It is what psychologist Chris Argyris describes as the difference between "single-loop" and "double-loop" learning - attacking the symptoms rather than the disease.

To avoid making assumptions, remember the adage that "the mind is like a parachute - it works best when it's open."

4. HAVE CLEAR OBJECTIVES

The leadership literature is laden with references to visions and vision-aries. No one doubts that Martin Luther King had a vision when he said "I have a dream ..." in 1963, or that Mahatma Gandhi had a vision of an India freed from British control, or that Nelson Mandela had a vision of a South Africa freed from apartheid. But in the real, nitty-gritty world of business, few leaders are on moral crusades of the sort that truly merit the word "vision."

Needing visionaries who have visions is part of the hype and jargon that can obscure what leadership means. Think instead of clear-sighted leaders, who can picture an opportunity, or something better, or even successfully different. Such leaders articulate their goal or objective in such a way that others can understand it – they are then able to persuade people to join with them in achieving it.

In 1981, Jack Welch had a clear picture of what he wanted GE to become, but he didn't call it a vision. Instead, he established clear objectives (see Chapter 7) and even set 20-year goals – for instance, that 25% of GE's revenue would come from new markets in China, India, and Mexico by the year 2000.

Effective leadership means having clear objectives – without them, nobody can see what to do or achieve.

5. BE DECISIVE

The leadership mantle is not an easy one to wear. One of the burdens it brings with it is that, as President Truman's desktop motto said, "the buck stops here." Prevarication and indecisiveness do not go hand-in-hand with effective leadership.

But to act decisively should not be mistaken as a need to act fast. A decision to decide later is, if it's for the right reasons, a valid decision of itself. Each situation brings with it its own complexities, considerations, and unknowns. Recourse to the right advice, listening to alternative arguments, weighing up the facts, may all be necessary preludes to making a final judgment. To decide in haste and then repent at leisure is an uncomfortable experience.

There could have been few more testing times for a decision-making leadership than the Cuban missile crisis that confronted President

Kennedy in 1961. Over 13 days, the world teetered on the edge of nuclear conflagration. Yet, having learned his lessons from the US invasion of Cuba during the Bay of Pigs fiasco six months earlier, Kennedy this time held back from precipitate action, encouraged wide and open debate, listened to advice from all quarters, and only then took the series of critical decisions that he knew were his alone to make. Throughout, he was under the spotlight of the world's media and faced considerable pressure, especially from the US military, to act hard and fast.

Alongside decisiveness comes courage, commitment, and perseverance in following through decisions made. There are, of course, no prizes for continuing to back a wrong decision when it is obvious that this is the case, but showing determination and steely resolve in support of the right decision is essential. Personal popularity is not a necessary ingredient in business leadership – however much we may want it.

6. CHOOSE THE RIGHT PEOPLE

One skill that effective leaders have is an ability to pick the right people to have around them. This is not an inborn talent, but an acquired one. To be a good judge of people requires many characteristics already mentioned: the use of experience, good observation and listening, an open mind, well-directed – often probing – questioning. Put together, this may seem to become inherently intuitive, but while the high use of intuition is a personality trait, assessing people is a developable skill. People who shrug their shoulders and admit to being poor judges of character have a lot to learn if they want to become leaders.

But it's not just about choosing the right people – it's about putting them in the right jobs or giving them the right responsibilities. Here, knowing yourself plays another vital role – building an effective team to support successful leadership involves weighing up the strengths and weaknesses of *all* involved. Leaders such as Akio Morita and Archie Norman found people with whom they developed a very powerful co-leadership relationship (see Chapter 7).

Quite apart from the leadership team, it is important to identify talent throughout the organization. That talent can come in many forms – but seeking out and developing people is a vital leadership role. They may become today's change agents or tomorrow's generation of top leaders. For example, GE has an enviable record, finding – as someone put it – "eight Jack Welches in a row, all home-grown," and Welch himself is proud of both the leadership talent that remains within GE and those who have moved on to leadership roles elsewhere.

7. DEVOLVE POWER

"Empowerment" is another management word that's been ground into the dust by inappropriate use or overuse. But the original concept behind it holds good.

There is little point, after all, in finding the right people and attracting those with talent, only to hang on to the reins of power. In flattened, increasingly networked organizations, power has to be diffused and delegated if it is to be effective. But this is not something that can happen overnight – even though many thought it could.

Devolving power means that those to whom it is given have to have been prepared for the leadership roles that they incur. It is totally unrealistic to believe that those who have become accustomed to centralized control will suddenly blossom into good decision-makers. Some will, but many won't. Archie Norman "released" – dismissed or accepted the resignations of – those Asda store managers who couldn't cope with the need to manage change at the local levels (see Chapter 7). But in a less crisis-ridden situation, good leadership develops and mentors new leaders at all levels, so that they are prepared for responsibility when it comes.

Many people find it extremely uncomfortable to relinquish power to others. After all, it is access to the levers of power that is a driving force for many business people. So it is difficult, but by no means impossible, to switch to being mentor, supporter, facilitator, and teacher. Indeed, those who can do so experience a very different – probably more satisfying – sense of fulfillment (the top end of Maslow's hierarchy of needs – see Chapter 8).

In a highly complex world many things, from potentially new strategic directions to dramatic changes in levels of customer service, are more likely to be found nearer the edges of the organization than at the boardroom table or in a strategic planning document.

8. LEAD BY EXAMPLE

A critical leadership issue, but one that does not take too much explanation. It is part of human nature to adopt role models, people we set up as exemplars of what we do, or don't, wish to become. From our earliest days, parents, teachers, friends, all provide us with models we choose to follow or reject.

To set an example means setting standards and abiding by them. Failure to do so creates a collapse in credibility from which few leaders can recover. The more striking the change in behavior or attitude that you want to create, the more you have to become living evidence of how it is to be done and why it is worthwhile.

9. ACT WITH INTEGRITY

Although closely aligned to example-setting, the need to act with integrity is sufficiently different to merit its own entry. Integrity is being honest. It is about having strong moral principles. To act with integrity means acting ethically, and often openly. It means acting for a wider cause, not out of self-interest. It is the basis for trust.

There is much about business today that can raise questions about a leader's integrity – bonuses and stock options can appear to create powerful motives for acting self-interestedly. On many occasions during the 1980s and 1990s, share prices rose in direct proportion to the numbers of workers being laid off – enriching the corporate leaders, through their options, while thousands of employees faced the hardship of unemployment. By no means were all such leaders the "fat cats" they were demonized to be. But people like Al "Chainsaw" Dunlap, who literally destroyed companies like Sunbeam while making himself a personal fortune, did huge damage to the respect in which corporate leadership is held. Visible integrity and high ethical standards are needed more now than ever before.

Peter Drucker recommends the "mirror test." Leaders should make sure that the person they see in the mirror every morning is the person they want to be, to respect, to believe in.

10. KNOW WHEN TO GO

However good we are, or believe ourselves to be, there is always a need for new blood and fresh ideas. Earlier success can make us cling to something that is well past its sell-by date. Henry Ford resisted any changes to his *Model T* for 19 years between 1908 and 1927, even kicking one modified model to pieces in front of everyone. This despite the fact that General Motors were rapidly eating into Ford's market share.

But many leaders find it difficult, sometimes impossible, to let go. Arnold Weinstock ran GEC in the UK for 33 years, in the end building up a cash mountain because he couldn't think of good things to spend it on (see Chapter 1). Armand Hammer, in his capacity as chairman and CEO, ran Occidental Petroleum as his own personal fiefdom for 35 years.

Leaders, at all levels, need to know when it is time to pass over the reins to someone new, ideally someone that will be as good as, if not better than, they have been. Many leaders want to leave a legacy but, by overstaying their time, they often leave precisely the wrong sort of legacy.

KEY LEARNING POINTS

Leading is not easy, but these ten steps provide a good basis for success.

1 Know yourself.
2 And go on learning.
3 Don't assume anything.
4 Have clear objectives.
5 Be decisive.
6 Choose the right people.
7 Devolve power.
8 Lead by example.
9 Act with integrity.
10 Know when to go.

Frequently Asked Questions (FAQs)

Q1: What is leadership?

A: There is no single answer, but an introduction to the subject can be found in Chapter 1, followed in Chapter 2 by a look at some of the definitions of leadership which have been put forward by key thinkers in the subject.

Q2: Why is leadership so important?

A: The case study in Chapter 1, looking at the contrasting fates of two long-established industrial giants – General Electric and GEC/Marconi – pointedly illustrates the importance of leadership.

Q3: Are leaders born or made?

A: While there have been examples of "natural born leaders" throughout history, such people are rare and the current consensus of thinking is that leaders *can* be made. See, for example, "Leaders in the real world," Chapter 2 and "'Great man' and 'trait' theory," Chapter 3.

Q4: Why do some leaders go badly wrong?

A: For four examples of why, and how, some leaders go wrong, see "The dark side of leadership," Chapter 8. See also "the neurotic organization," Chapter 6, for some psychological characteristics of bad leaders which can have seriously detrimental effects on an organization and the people within it.

Q5: Do successful leaders need to be charismatic?

A: Many believe that charisma is a valuable, but not essential, characteristic in a leader – though such a characteristic is not without its downsides. See "The charisma enigma," Chapter 6.

Q6: What does globalization mean for leaders and leadership?

A: Globalization brings with it issues of cross-cultural understanding, international relationships, workforce diversity, ethics, and multicultural communications, to name but a few. How leaders deal with these issues is critical. For ideas on how this should (and shouldn't) be done, see Chapter 5 generally, and, for a shining example of how it can be done, see "Best practice – ABB's global leaders" in that chapter.

Q7: Do effective leaders do it all single-handedly?

A: In today's highly complex organizations it is increasingly difficult for one person alone to run things from the top and there is growing awareness of the value of co-leading with somebody who has complementary skills and abilities. See "Co-leadership," Chapter 6, and, for some examples of co-leadership in practice, Chapter 7.

Q8: Why is Jack Welch always being held up as a good leader?

A: In the detailed study in Chapter 7 you can find out why this legendary transformer has become a role model for many other leaders around the world and why, amongst many other accolades, he has been voted "Manager of the Century."

Q9: How do I find out more about the subject?

A: A selection of the many available resources can be found in Chapter 9, including leadership centers/foundations, books, journals, and Websites.

Q10: What things can make a leader successful?

A: Leading is not easy, but Chapter 10 describes 10 steps which, although they cannot of themselves *make* someone a leader, will certainly provide a good basis for success.

Index

9 781841 123592